BRAND

is a four letter word

BRAND

is a four letter word

Positioning and The Real Art of Marketing.

Austin McGhie

Published by Advantage, Charleston, South Carolina.
Member of Advantage Media Group.

ADVANTAGE is a registered trademark and the Advantage colophon is a trademark of Advantage Media Group, Inc.

Printed in the United States of America.

ISBN: 978-159932-327-5
LCCN: 2012933449

This publication is designed to provide accurate and authoritative information in regard to the subject matter covered. It is sold with the understanding that the publisher is not engaged in rendering legal, accounting, or other professional services. If legal advice or other expert assistance is required, the services of a competent professional person should be sought.

TreeNeutral

Advantage Media Group is proud to be a part of the Tree Neutral® program. Tree Neutral offsets the number of trees consumed in the production and printing of this book by taking proactive steps such as planting trees in direct proportion to the number of trees used to print books. To learn more about Tree Neutral, please visit www.treeneutral.com. To learn more about Advantage's commitment to being a responsible steward of the environment, please visit www.advantagefamily.com/green

Acknowledgements

Before I start thanking people who have helped me along the way, I'd like to acknowledge two people who wrote a book years ago. A book that started me down a path that inevitably led to the writing of this book of mine. The book was "Positioning: The Battle for your Mind" and the authors were Jack Trout and Al Ries. Thirty years later, this book still has a special place in my mind. In many ways, I've spent the years since rolling their ideas around in my mind, finding ways to use them and make them my own. Jack was kind enough to write a foreword to my book, though I'm not sure that he fully appreciates the profound impact his ideas had on a young brand manager just getting started up the ladder. Thank you.

Now, on a more personal note, I'll start at the beginning. I'd like to thank Jos Wintermans for offering me my first job (at Standard/Nabisco Brands in Toronto) when I was a fresh-faced MBA. While I'd like to think he saw promise in me, this may just have been an act of sympathy. Don Herron was my first boss and passed on his love of debate, along with the idea that marketing was just one big puzzle. Mike Dawson, a peer (though each of us was certain he was smarter than the other), showed me that this work thing shouldn't be taken too seriously.

Don Fritz hired me away to Kellogg's, and then from Canada to Australia, from where Kellogg's ran most of Asia. Don is, without a doubt, the toughest son of a bitch I will ever work for. He is also the best boss I ever had. While in Australia, I had the good fortune of hiring David McKay, who went on to become Kellogg's CEO. He reminded me that I once told him he wasn't that great a marketer—but that we'd all end up working for him some day. (To be fair, he was a really good marketer.) Australia was life changing for me. We took a declining, unprofitable company and increased our market share to the point where our competitors began to leave the market. I loved our team there and thank all of them for helping make this period five of the best years of my life. Even more important, I met my wife in Australia, our son was born there and my daughter's name is Sydney. Great years indeed.

Once we decided to move to Chicago, I ran across this guy named Bruce Beach who ran Ogilvy & Mather, the ad agency I had always aspired to work for. As an Army Ranger, Bruce earned several Purple Hearts in Vietnam. As an agency head, Bruce was fearless enough to hire a young guy with no ad or retail experience to run the Sears account, O&M's single largest account at the time. When he left six months later he pushed me into his old job. Bruce is a brand with a lot of differentiated advantage, and I'll always owe him. I also owe Graham Philips, O&M chairman at the time, for looking after the guy who found himself in deeper waters than expected.

Ultimately, our boss was Sir Martin Sorrell, whom I had the good fortune of meeting a few times. While he may have his detractors, the fact is that he is smarter, works harder and has more strength of will than any of them. I'm still not sure I liked working for him, but if you don't respect what he has accomplished you really don't get it.

Then there was Peter Georgescu, chairman of Young & Rubicam, who epitomizes old-school advertising royalty in an incredibly smart, energetic and almost mesmerizing way. He won me over at some private club in New York with an average membership age of 105. Peter and his wife gave their lives over to the agency he ran, and I wanted to be just like him if I ever grew up. At Y&R, Ed Vick showed me that agency heads could be tough and Peter Stringham showed me that they didn't need to be, and I thank them both.

All of which leads to the most fun I've ever had in business— becoming a partner at Sterling Brands. What we do, our clients and our people, make work fun. So much fun that I feel a sort of guilt—surely it must be tougher than this? I want to thank all our clients. Yes, we like your business but, more important, most of you have made this a great place to work. I have learned from you all. Many of the people who work for me have been with me from the start, back when we inherited an unprofitable, small strategy business that looked like nothing more than an adjunct to our design business. Thank you for allowing me to look forward to coming to work . . . almost every day.

I also want to thank Debbie Millman, who in addition to being a partner and a friend, represents a target I may never reach. When I arrived at Sterling, I told Deb I would do everything possible to make our strategy business as successful as her design business. While we're closer than ever, she just keeps moving that line away from me.

My last professional thank you goes to Simon Williams, founder and chairman of Sterling Brands. When Simon hired me I thought I'd do the job for a year and then return to a respectable job client-side. Ten years later, here I am. He's the only boss who ever called me up to tell me he loved me. He's the heart and soul of the business I work in, and we all love him for it. I once told Simon that if he didn't want to have a long dinner with a senior candidate then he shouldn't hire that person. (It's what's known as the dinner test.) After all these years working together, Simon still passes the dinner test.

My thanks to all those I have worked with and been influenced by. For better and for worse, you're all in here somewhere.

Of course, none of these acknowledgements have anything to do with writing a book. Or do they? Specific thanks for this book go to Simon for his encouragement, and to Joe DiNucci and Atiya Davidson for pushing me to get it done. Joe actually went as far as to place it on his personal "bucket list," an honor of which I'm clearly unworthy. An early draft was edited by Joel Raphaelson, a colleague of David Ogilvy and a truly gifted writer. Joel and his wife, Marikay, are two of the most interesting people I've had the great pleasure of knowing. A later draft was edited by Mike Malone, a ruthlessly honest critic who did a great job of pointing out my writing tics and adding value from start to finish.

Most of all, I want to thank my wife Sara. To make a long story short, Sara is the main reason—maybe the only reason—I lead a happy, fulfilled life. I do not want to even consider where I would be if I hadn't found her. We have two amazing and accomplished kids, Andy and Sydney, and I look forward to driving home across the Golden Gate Bridge every single weeknight.

TABLE OF CONTENTS

Opening Rant

I'm sick and tired of the B word. *Branding.*

It has to be the most misused—and least understood—word in the business of . . . well, *branding.*

Let's start from the top: unless you're a cattle rancher, there's no such thing as "branding." If you are a marketing professional, you are dealing with a noun, not a verb, a consequence, not an action.

Simply put: you can't brand something. You can *earn* that designation, but you can't just do it. A brand is a prize, an award—one that can only be bestowed upon you by the marketplace.

If I already sound grumpy, here at the very beginning of my book, it's because the B word, never precisely defined in the first place, has become such a nebulous, fit-everything term that it now essentially has no meaning. Worse, it is regularly abused by marketing people as a means of extracting money from clients and bullying skeptics into silence.

Building a brand is a strategy, not an objective. Sometimes it's the right strategy, and sometimes it's not. Let's stop blindly worshipping the B word. The sooner we marketers demystify this single word, the sooner our business partners will trust us with the car keys.

It is time to get back to first principles, to establish what "brand" is and what it is not, and to restore to the concept the value it might have to someone who actually practices the art of marketing.

So, let's begin with a true definition of brand.

Whatever you've been taught, here's the truth: You have a *thing*—a product, service, idea, person (including yourself), place, etc. This something can have an image, a reputation and/or a track record. But it can only be a *brand* once it reaches a particular destination, and not a minute before. The most interesting feature of that destination is that you don't know where it is until you get there. No one can give you a schedule, or an estimated time of arrival. You arrive when your audience tells you that you have arrived, when your audience tells you that you have, indeed, built a brand.

No matter what so-called "branding" professionals may tell you, there's no magic line to cross. There is no line in the sand with "brand" written on one side and "product" on the other. It would be convenient if there were—but real marketing is anything and everything but convenient.

So what the hell is a brand in the first place?

The actual definitions of brand are almost as numerous and varied as the people who are trying to sell their "branding" services to you. My favorite: *A brand is emotional shorthand for a wealth of accumulated or assumed information.* An even simpler definition is that *a brand is present when the value of what a product, service or personality **means** to its audience is greater than the value of what it **does** for that audience.*

I like these definitions, but there's still a problem. I can't even get my own colleagues to agree upon a single definition of brand. And yet your company and thousands of others are being asked to spend billions of dollars each year in pursuit of this nebulous and elusive concept.

So, here is how we will begin. Pick your own definition of brand. But whatever you choose, the important thing is that you always treat that term as a noun. Promise me you will never, ever use it as a verb. From now on, you will look upon brand as the prize at the end of a long road. That road itself comes in many shapes and sizes. It can be short or long, wide or narrow, straight or curved. It can also be well traveled, which helps you to find your way, but it's the lonely, less traveled roads that carry the greatest long-term potential. And it's the lonely roads that create the brands we all love to use (with the benefit of 20/20 hindsight) as case studies.

But if brand is forever the noun, what then is the verb? What is the work of marketing?

Positioning.

Marketing is, in short, the art of positioning. And whatever your *thing*, the marketer's job is to position an idea of that thing, its emotional shorthand, with sufficient power and consistency over time so that the audience comes to see it as a brand. As salespeople know better than anyone, if you can't position something, you have no hope of selling it. But salespeople are all about selling, so they'll shift that position in five minutes if it helps to make the sale. They are masters of in-the-moment positioning. In contrast, marketers need to be masters of positions that can hold up over time, which is a different task altogether.

This means that the real challenge you face—the real work—is not building your brand, but rather in defining, clarifying, targeting, capturing and holding your *position.*

You can start by asking yourself a series of questions:

- How clear is our position? Can our customers explain it?

- More important, can all of our employees explain it?

- More important still, do they believe it?

- How unique is it?

- Does it create competitive advantage? Can we leverage it?

- How much cultural currency and momentum does it have?

Whatever it is you are selling, it needs to be reduced to a single idea that can stick in someone's head. It needs to stand out from all the noise and clutter of the marketplace. It needs to take on an importance inside that customer's head that outweighs any functional benefit it might provide. Most of all, your position must be an idea that will actually *matter*.

Many companies, even some we consider strong brands, are basically incapable of presenting their position in a simple, cogent way. Why? For starters, the senior management teams at these companies have a lot more to think about than I do, and the odds are high that none of them got where they are because of their positioning expertise. They all know the B word and that a strong brand has value, but most find the whole discussion nebulous and lacking the specificity of other discussions that go on within their enterprise.

It's ironic that we tell entrepreneurs that they need to have a short, well thought-out statement of their business, technology and market positioning (the legendary elevator pitch) if they have any hope of obtaining money from venture capitalists. And yet once they secure that money and are underway, it never seems to cross their minds—not for decades, sometimes—that they need to regularly update that pitch in order to obtain money from their current source of cash: customers.

If you haven't fully thought out your positioning and viewed it through your customers' eyes, you are already in a dangerous and vulnerable position. Forget "branding"; you need to sit down with your team *right now* and ponder just who you are . . . and then make sure that the result is congruent with your current business strategy.

Positioning happens. That's a given. But if you don't assert your position very forcibly, others (particularly competitors) are only too happy to do it for you.

This will help: A great position is a simple yet compelling idea that represents an area of differentiated advantage. It establishes what it is that makes you different from your competitors, and does it in a way that creates a competitive advantage in the eyes of the customers or consumers you serve. Think of your position as the front door to your house. Inside that house is everything you do, and you're justifiably proud of it. But you first need to get me inside your front door to appreciate what you've got. So what's the idea that will pull me through your door and away from someone else's house? What's the one idea for which you want to become famous?

There are many things you must do well to succeed. Some are absolutely critical to that success. But which of them represent real differences? Of those that are truly unique, which can be made to define you in a way that will work to your competitive advantage? Be ruthless with yourself—be brutally honest in your self-appraisal—and you'll find the idea that can come to represent you in a way that creates differentiated advantage.

In practical terms, a position is really a distilled and concise representation of a marketing strategy. At the heart of any good marketing strategy is the creation of differentiated advantage. The words of a positioning idea therefore represent the most compressed articulation of that strategy of differentiated advantage.

Ideally, this position also represents a strong, even provocative, point of view. A point of view you could write on a whiteboard and not be laughed out of the room—one around which you could actually write an interesting white paper. Ideally, this statement is one that would inspire your fellow employees to nod and say, "Yeah, that's us," and cause your competitors to cover their mouths and whisper, "Oh, shit . . ."

But it is not enough to be merely clever or insightful. Positioning has nothing to do with communication. A successful position must be built on what you do, not on what you say. If everyone in the room reads your position statement and thinks, "That's not us," or "God, if that were only true," you have failed the brutal honesty test and no amount of creative communication can help you.

In other words, unless you can *be* it, don't say it—especially in this age of digital transparency. A true position is an asset that drives internal behavior throughout the organization. Ideally, it is a lodestar for your company: it gives the organization a sense of purpose and direction—and then, by extension, transmits that same sense of purpose to your audience. If your positioning isn't guiding the product development people, no amount of clever marketing can credibly convey it to your customers. Ducks that talk like swans are nothing more than well-spoken ducks.

Further, your position must be built upon a set of pillars or filters that help the position properly channel and guide behavior. If the position doesn't guide and inspire the organization—the *entire* organization—it has no hope of guiding and inspiring the consumer. As Gandhi said, "be the change you wish to see in the world." Positioning is the *attainable change* you wish to see in your enterprise.

"Okay," some of you may be saying, "but hold on a minute." Branding? Positioning? Isn't the difference between the two terms just a matter of semantics?

Yes—but no! Because of the attitudes and behaviors they drive, these terms are more different than everyday language suggests. Although this opening rant is an attack on the idea of "branding," brands are real. Their value can be measured. Brands are initiatives that have built value over and above function. Strong brands sell more than similarly priced weak brands. Strong brands are more profitable than weak brands. Strong brands recruit better employees. Strong brands hold their stock price better than weak brands. And strong brands can be astonishingly resilient. (Just ask Apple.)

To repeat (something people tend to do in books and in rants): A strong brand is a marketplace *response*, not a marketer's stimulus. It's the prize. I'll continue to use the word brand throughout this book, because that prize is an incredibly valuable asset and we've all grown up using this moniker to describe it. But I solemnly swear to never utter the B word again as a verb—unless I'm still ranting against it.

Marketers do stuff. If your stuff is more compelling and fresh than your competitor's stuff, you will sell more in the short run. If your stuff stays compelling and fresh and is held together by a consistent position over time, you will sell a lot more in the long term.

Positioning is hard work. Positioning is process. And positioning never stands in isolation. It can only exist within a marketing strategy.

When expressed externally to your target audience, positioning must travel through the very complex medium of the human mind. And only if you really understand that medium can you possibly hope to create a stimulus (expression) that can both navigate it and still get the desired response (the position). This medium is always changing and it contains both competitors and friends—along with their differing perspectives, hopes, fears and secrets. It also holds both true and false "facts." Positioning is part art, part science and part psychology, and that's why marketing strategy is a lot harder than it looks, especially if you actually want to win.

So while we continue to appreciate great brands and their architects, let's stop talking about "branding." Instead, let's focus the discussion on positioning and execution. Let's focus on the stimulus and not the response. Let's focus on the work required, rather than the prize awarded, because it's the work that we marketers toil over day in and day out. Let's reduce the mystique and bullshit surrounding the notion of "branding" and instead build a more practical guide to positioning and execution.

With that, let's begin by understanding what this book is about:

- It's a practical guide for people who like to think of themselves as marketers
- It's about positioning that guides and inspires your organization, and then guides and inspires your audience
- It's about finding, understanding and growing your audience

- It's about two-way communication with that audience to bring the position to life—over time and by working together
- It's about actively de-positioning brands and ideas you compete against
- It's about difference—real difference that creates advantage
- It's about reality-based brand building
- It's about the importance of doing first, talking second
- It's about attention—the real currency of marketing
- It's about building critical marketing mass
- It's about building your brand
- It's about winning

But it's not—ever—about "branding."

BRAND IS A
FOUR-LETTER WORD

1

An Introduction

"The future is here.
It's just not widely
distributed yet."

—*William Gibson, writer*

The need to position your product or service so as to differentiate it in ways that create competitive advantage has not and will not change over time. How you accomplish this, however, is where all the change resides.

If you've been working in the industry for the past ten years you've witnessed and participated in a fascinating decade from a marketing perspective. From heart-breaking failure to spectacular success and all that lies in between, everything has been magnified, sped up and colored more brightly. These are amazing times we're living in. But they're also fearful times.

We will look back on these years as not merely a period of change, but also of complete upheaval. And in the marketing profession, we'll talk about the pre-technology era—those years before technology fundamentally changed society and thus the business of marketing.

The Internet is proving itself to be the single most powerful change agent the world has ever seen. It is inspiring radical cultural and political shifts all around us. It has helped overturn bad ideas and bad governments. And it has fundamentally changed how we relate to one another. Marketing doesn't stand a chance.

For those of us in the business of marketing (particularly those of us over forty) these are indeed the best and worst of times. It's as if sometime in the mid '90s all of us were unknowingly transported to a new and very different place. Many of us still have a bit of vertigo from the trip; others are still refusing to look out the window at the changed landscape. Thank God for denial—it's been keeping many of us sane.

But for those who have looked out the window, both with dread and with a genuine fascination for this strange new marketing landscape, it is now long-since time for us to get out there and figure out how to survive. Most of our time-honored principles look as if they will still apply, at least conceptually, though often in wildly different new applications. Other areas of the game appear to have irrevocably changed—so much so that those of us at mid-career may never again grasp the game in a completely intuitive and natural way.

Marketing hasn't died in this new world. Instead, like most things, it has adapted and is evolving in a new direction whose ultimate destination is unknowable. As the interface between provider and consumer, marketing will always be a central business discipline. Brands will always carry real economic value. But beyond that, almost everything to do with marketing is in extreme flux. You might even say that everything is all fluxed up.

This book is written for marketers of all shapes and sizes. Its goal is to balance the important and consistent principle of positioning with the rapidly changing environment within which the marketer must create and nurture that position. If you have just entered the marketing profession and are young and in tune with the zeitgeist, your initial impression will likely be that some of the established practices described here are hopelessly anachronistic. But give them a chance; there's a reason they've been successful for so long. Similarly, a marketing veteran might find some of the new ideas in this book utterly insane. But look around you: it's an insane world right now, and great marketers have always been able to create order out of chaos.

Officially or unofficially, we marketers have always had a rulebook. The old rulebook, consisting of unwritten rules, legends, case studies and proven tricks, was written primarily by Procter & Gamble, the greatest consumer marketing company of the twentieth century, and the application of this rulebook took place largely in relatively uncluttered marketplaces. Those marketplaces lacked transparency insofar as the target audience was concerned, and were filled with one-way, hard-to-avoid communication as to why one product was better than another. Persuasion was the order of the day.

The twenty-first-century marketing rulebook will be much less supermarket-centric and will be less about rules and more about suggestions. Whether we know it or not, that book is being written right now, although many of us are just using the first few pages. But keep in mind that the mavericks who break rules and ignore suggestions often build the most spectacularly successful businesses and brands (or create the biggest business disasters). You can talk about difference or you can just *be* different.

As I said earlier, marketing is all about positioning. Fortunes rise and fall based on your ability to devise a truly great position and then take that position to the marketplace in a compelling and fresh way each day. This is real-life marketing and, as appealing as marketing theory can be, it is the day-to-day work of establishing a position and defending and growing it that ultimately writes the best chapters in the rulebook.

> ## "In theory, there is no difference between theory and practice; in practice, there is."
>
> *—Chuck Reid*

We in the brand business tend to be our own worst enemies. We seem to love soft, artistic language that leaves real business people wondering if we have a practical bone in our body. We are different. We should seem different. But we have to connect our thinking more clearly to that of the business it must support. We need to convey that thinking in terms that others can actually understand. If our language doesn't seem real to these businesses, how can our thinking be put into practice?

We in the brand business also love our constructs. My colleagues who read this will chuckle, as I may in fact be the world's most prolific creator of useless constructs. Some of these constructs (positioning, for example) are incredibly useful, but the last time I checked, the daily business of marketing just doesn't easily fit into any single conceptual framework. The day-to-day reality of a marketer actually remains pretty random in nature.

Writing this book is a perfect example: I just pulled together all the thoughts that have been racing unchecked through my head, organized them and then studied the resulting pile of paper to see if it was structured enough and weighed enough to be called a book. Could order emerge from chaos?

I have idea ADD, hence the short chapters. You can read them all in one sitting or you can snack. Overall, my aim is to be as provocatively practical as possible. You be the judge.

2

Brand (Double) Speak

"Philosophy is a battle
against the bewitchment
of intelligence by
means of language."
—*Ludwig Wittgenstein,*
twentieth-century philosopher

The business of brand strategy is stuffed with enough esoteric concepts and words to drive you crazy. So before I get too far into this book, here's an attempt to define and explain six key and interrelated components of marketing strategy. With any luck, this should also correspond to how I've used these ideas throughout the book.

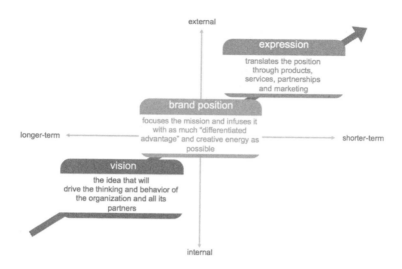

Vision

- *The idea that drives the organization.* Vision is the reason a company's employees come to work every day. This vision must work actively to imbue the organization—and by extension, its strategy—with a clear sense of purpose. Better still, with a sense of mission. This vision must also have utility. It must inform all decision-making, including marketing strategy and, therefore, positioning.

- *Must be deeply internalized.* Most companies don't spend nearly enough time ensuring their vision paints a clear picture for their people.

- *Weak vision = weak brand.* Smart and creative marketing may delay the inevitable, but a business without a strong vision is ultimately a brand fighting to stay afloat.

- *What business are you in?* It all starts with that disarmingly simple question. Apple's answer to this question transformed the company, while Yahoo! still has to answer this question if it is to have any hope of success.

Strong, vision-driven organizations

- Visa has been working hard to replace paper with plastic; ultimately, it wants to replace both with smart devices. Everyone wins in the world Visa hopes to create—consumers, banks and, of course, Visa itself.

- While consumer electronics companies are scrambling to harness technology, Apple has moved from technology to entertainment, from fascinating computers to irreplaceable and constant companions. Its vision (devices matter) is increasingly in direct conflict with the Amazon vision (dumb device, intelligence in the cloud), and while both can still prosper, only one worldview can be right. While I might have bet on the Amazon vision, recent experience with an amazing device (my iPhone 4S) and a disappointing device (Kindle Fire) has me rethinking things.

- Google wants to organize the world's information. How's that for a vision?

Business Model

- *A strong and differentiated business model* is the most effective of all marketing tools. If your business is differentiated, your brand will ultimately be differentiated. Obviously, marketers can build highly differentiated brands out of non-differentiated businesses, but the degree of difficulty is so much higher.

- It's hard to see how you can have a strong and differentiated business model without an equally *strong and differentiated sense of vision behind it.* On the other hand, a strong vision doesn't need a highly differentiated business model to succeed.

- Whereas Wal-Mart's business model is deeply entrenched, highly differentiated and creates differentiated advantage, most packaged goods brands lack this luxury and have to *create difference* at the product and marketing communication level.

Strong, nearly unassailable business models

- You can certainly out-communicate Wal-Mart and Southwest, but good luck to you if you think you can compete directly with them when it comes to their business models. While I tend to believe marketing can win any war, these are not competitors I'd like to test my conviction on.

- You can compete with McDonald's, but unless you can actively "de-position" it in some sustained way, the company's operational excellence will wear you down over time. Operational excellence doesn't sound unassailable, but finding an Achilles heel when it comes to companies like these is way harder than most people realize.

- Amazon has—relatively quietly—placed itself into a position from which it can attack new markets. That elevated position also means that competitors will have great difficulty scaling the walls of Amazon.com.

- But nothing is unassailable. Look at Boeing: it killed off all competition only to find that European governments were willing to come together and bankroll a new competitor.

Business Strategy

- Driven by the vision and business model, the business strategy is the *blueprint* that outlines how you will go to market.

- Exactly how will you deploy the business model in a way that creates *sustainable competitive advantage?* How will you create and deploy products and services? How will you support that deployment?

Marketing Strategy

- Driven by the vision, business model and strategy, the best way to compete in the marketplace is through the intelligent use of marketing. If, by analogy, your business model and strategy are your Order of Battle (i.e., your army, its resources and how you will deploy your troops) your marketing strategy is closer to the *territory* over which you will fight, whom you will fight and how you will take that fight to them in order to win.

- Keep in mind that building a brand is *not mandatory*. Building a brand is a strategy, not an objective.

Clever Marketing Strategy

- ESPN wrote the book on this one. <u>Combine a niche you can own with an attitude that shows you own it.</u> Stay true to your strategy and keep it fresh—year after year. While this is easy to say, it's remarkably hard to do.

- Starbucks built itself as a "third place" rather than a coffee retailer. It also understood the importance of a happy barista. The rest is history.

- Target knew it couldn't assail Wal-Mart on price, so it introduced a line of name designers dedicated to creating "cheap-chic."

- When Fox News decided to focus on an audience that perceived itself as underserved when it came to media, it became an opinion leader for the right. You may not love the network's politics, but you have to admire its marketing savvy.

- Pepsi just couldn't beat Coke—until someone realized Pepsi was sweeter and could beat Coke in a blind taste test. The "Pepsi Taste Test" made history, partly because it was smart marketing strategy and partly because the other guy blinked.

Position

- This is the one *idea*, or perspective, that you must champion through everything that you do, both internally and externally. It is the idea that will represent you in the marketplace. And whereas you don't have to have a brand to succeed, you must have a position to do so.

- Needless to say, there's a lot of pressure on how you position yourself. A position must represent the vision of the company and it must leverage the business model. It must be a *distilled representation* of the marketing strategy. It must stay true to the customer experience. And most of all, it must be an idea that can guide and inspire the organization, as well as guide and inspire your audience.

- The more your position is driven by a credible sense of mission the better. People may buy brands that don't have a sense of mission, but they will *participate* in brands that do.

Intelligent Positioning

- Dove and Axe, both owned by Unilever, are great examples of style over substance—and I mean this as a compliment to their marketers. Dove saw that women were sick and tired of the lookalike (read: beautiful and waif-like) models used to promote beauty brands, and presented us with "Real Beauty." I'm very proud that Sterling Brands helped the brand get there but I would be the first to admit that "there" wouldn't be nearly as significant if Ogilvy hadn't absolutely nailed the communications side of things. Similarly, Axe grokked young men and built a highly successful brand out of thin air by simply bringing the teen male to life in every dimension of its brand communication mix.

- In the 1970s, 7-Up successfully positioned itself as "The Uncola," only to switch agencies and completely lose the script. It confused position with execution, and instead of keeping the position and freshening the execution, dumped the baby out with the bathwater.

- On the other hand, Levi's continues to want to deny who it is. Its mantra seems to be: "Young people don't find us cool and they wouldn't be caught dead in most of the retailers that carry us—but let's make them our marketing focus anyway." And while Levi's fights this uphill battle, Lee and Wrangler walk away with Middle America.

Communication

- Presenting your position to your audience in a way that assures its attention is more difficult than many marketers seem to realize. It's easy to communicate an idea to someone who is paying attention. It's remarkably tough to accurately communicate an idea in a way that *captures the attention* of someone who doesn't care. And by and large, you have to assume that your customers do not care.

- As we'll discuss, position drives communication. Communication is a *stimulus* designed to operate in a cultural medium in order to elicit the desired response. The desired response is the position. A simple closed loop—except for one critical factor. People process that stimulus in wildly different ways. What you say is seldom what they actually hear.

Impactful Communication

- Corona's ongoing campaign to find new and interesting ways to take us to the beach has done a remarkable job of selling the brand. The "Most Interesting Man in the World" campaign has done the same for Dos Equis.

- As the Old Spice Guy, ex-NFL player and actor Isaiah Mustafa has actually made Old Spice cool for the first time in its life.

- But for ongoing communication excellence, it's hard to get past Nike and its ad agency, Wieden-Kennedy. Time after time, they have managed to hit the creative ball out of the park, all the while maintaining that consistent thread you need to hold a brand together.

- And let's not forget Apple's "1984." One great ad, placed just once, and still being talked about to this day.

STRATEGY

A client recently asked me what I thought was the key to strategy. It was such a nebulous question that I had to really think about it—which meant that I mumbled an acceptable response and then went away and actually pondered it. I called the client later to say I had considered his question further and concluded that the most useful way to think about strategy was as the art of forced choice.

The art of forced choice. What the hell am I talking about?

When forming strategy, we are faced with a set of choices. They may not advertise themselves as choices, but those who are good at strategy see them this way. You have to separate the small decisions from the larger ones, make the small ones quickly, and seriously deliberate over the larger ones. These decisions are choices. There are usually several wrong choices, a few right choices and possibly one game-changing choice. While the time isn't always right to accept the higher risks inherent to a game-changer, the time is always right to know what those potential game changers might be.

In developing strategy our task is to gather all the input we need to drive strategic choice (otherwise known as research), then ensure that those choices are made in ways that create differentiated advantage. Every great position is the result of forced choice.

But here's the problem: most people don't like to make choices. Given the options of black or white, most people select gray. If you assume it's always better to be gray and part-right than to be white and boldly wrong (though I think we could have an interesting debate on this), you can understand why the middle ground is the strategic space most frequently occupied. Too many managers are afraid to get it wrong. Everyone wants to succeed, but few are bold enough to make their choices with the clarity and courage required to form great strategy.

So here's what you do: Assemble the choices facing you. Study them. Do whatever you need to make an intelligent decision. Then choose—keeping in mind that gray is an option only if mediocrity is the desired outcome.

Choose. Commit. Don't look back.

3

What the Hell is a Brand Anyway?

A brand is something
that won't come
off in the wash.

—Cowboy's adage

Now that we've driven the B word into a box, let's look inside that box.

Charles Revson, who founded and built Revlon, is often quoted as saying: "In the factory we make cosmetics, but in the drugstore we sell hope." In other words, companies and products build intellectual relationships while brands build emotional relationships. Consumers buy products but become emotionally invested in brands. Put yet another way, once consumers are emotionally vested, you have a brand.

Until this happens you do not have a brand. A product, regardless of how beautifully you package it, is still just a product—until you have built a brand. A name is just a name—until it earns the right to be called a brand name. A logo is just a pretty design—until it comes to represent something to its audience, intellectually and emotionally.

A simple economic definition might suggest that a brand is present when the value of what that product or service means to its audience is measurably greater than the value of what it does.

Once again, it's important to keep in mind that brands are collective marketplace responses, not marketing stimuli—a point that is often lost along the way. You can call it whatever you want, but it's not a brand until consumers collectively "tell you" it's a brand.

Let's revisit the definition with which we began this book:

> *A brand is a form of emotional shorthand for a wealth of accumulated and assumed knowledge.*

A little vague perhaps, but I like where it leads. In the good old days, a key function of brand was to act as a navigational device. In other words, why bother to find out the real story behind a product when you could simply trust its brand narrative. Fast-forward to today, and you can now get the entire story, all the facts (and lots of opinion too), with a few taps on any of your various digital devices.

I like my definition because it highlights the most profound change ever to hit the art of marketing. As product information becomes easier to access, emotional shorthand changes from being a simple and mostly subjective response to becoming the synecdoche for a vast amount of documentation that ultimately provokes a thoughtful decision. It is still ultimately a subjective choice, but the content and process of that choice is infinitely more complex than it used to be.

As I've said, brands are real. Brand value is real economic value. Brand strength builds market share. It provides pricing flexibility. It acts as a magnet for profitable partnerships. And sometimes it just gives marketers the time they need to get back on top of the situation.

Consider Apple. (Doesn't everyone in marketing?) The product became a brand. The brand became a badge. The badge became a cultural icon. Even after Apple completely marginalized itself, letting its consumer base down with a run of mediocre products, the icon endured. The brand gave the business the cushion of goodwill it needed to survive. Only when the company was "rebooted" (by the one person who understood the brand most intimately), could Apple again prosper.

Perhaps I'm stretching things a bit, but the Apple brand almost demanded that the company move into music and create the iPod. Did Steve Jobs listen to the demands of the brand, or were the demands of the brand simply an extension of his and his company's culture? Either way, it no longer mattered. Apple's brand, its culture and its products by then were seamlessly interwoven.

But a brand can only do so much. These days a brand simply cannot flourish for long unless it represents a truly useful product or service. Yes, you can be useful emotionally as well as rationally, but spontaneous access to information means there had better be some substance there somewhere. And at the end of the day, even a great brand can't flourish without a strong and viable business model.

Napster was an amazingly strong brand, built on an equally naïve business model. It just took too long for the company, in the face of ongoing litigation, to change its business model. By the time Napster resurfaced, its innocence was gone and too much time had passed.

TiVo also built a brand that became a cultural icon—to the point where TiVo even became a verb! But once again the business model and the marketing of the product doomed it to marginalization. For several very critical years company executives insisted on positioning the device as a cultural revolution, as an amazing piece of technology that would change the world. The problem is, real people don't buy cultural revolutions and they definitely don't buy scary technology. They buy simple, useful products they understand. Perhaps it wouldn't have mattered in the long run, as TiVo may have always been doomed to be a bridge technology. But if the company had assumed a simple consumer electronics stance with its product, rather than falling so deeply in love with its technology, perhaps TiVo could have built critical mass before industry forces went to work on it.

To use another example, consider the television networks. Once they were powerful brands, supported by viable, profitable business models. People actually identified with individual networks. But then came the remote control and the beginning of our viewing liberation. First we consumers mastered the channel change from the comfort of our sofa. Then along came cable and satellite and our choices exploded. And now Video on Demand is busy taking the dimension of time out of the equation.

We've gone from "What's on CBS?" to "When is *Glee* on?" and we're well on our way to "Let's just stream it." I'd argue that the big networks are no longer true brands and that, as content organizers, the role of networks today is closer to that of a developer and marketer. But the bottom line is that their old business model is simply not viable in the longer term. How, after all, can advertising-supported businesses prosper when everyone is skipping the ads?

The funny thing is that I've run across strong arguments to the contrary from some really smart marketers. They respond as if these developments are a bad thing. But it's just a reality, neither good nor bad. I'd argue that technology has made their jobs tougher, but also a lot more interesting. They aren't marketing a single brand anymore. That brand is becoming a name. A business, not a brand. And as a result, marketers are developing a wide range of products and services, many of which will become brands in their own right. Some of those brands are programs and some are people. Regardless, however, they all need to be positioned. Today, marketers must market those brands, in a variety of shapes and sizes and through a variety of channels—one of which happens to be a television set. Very cool!

Let's remind ourselves once again: A brand is a marketplace response, not a marketer's stimulus. You can't brand something. You can only position it.

- If you manage to create a position that is compelling, different and competitively advantageous, you're off to a good start

- If your organization has the ability to consistently execute to that position, you have a shot at becoming a successful brand

- If that position can stand the test of time, you have a shot at becoming a strong brand

- If that execution stays on strategy, is simple yet powerful, and is somehow kept fresh and surprising over time, you have a shot at becoming a great brand

- If you can do all of this better than your competition, your brand will win

Those are a lot of "ifs," but no one said this marketing thing is easy.

And at the very start of that chain of "ifs" is the notion of the right positioning. So how do you know if you've found the right position?

You know you've found the right position when your position is built around a single idea that:

- Is highly differentiated

- Creates competitive advantage

- Guides and inspires your organization and your audience

- Is sustainable over time

- Is provocative, even disruptive to the marketplace status quo

- Can be consistently executed over time, but in ways that evolve and stay fresh

That's a daunting list and few companies pull it off, which is why we all tend to use the same limited set of case studies (e.g., Apple, Nike, ESPN, Google, Starbucks). Marketing is positioning. Great marketing is positioning that fits all these criteria (and probably a few others I haven't articulated). Great marketing is the exception rather than the rule.

And you will need to work your butt off to become that exception.

4

Great Brands Are Built from the Inside.

If you can't get it right on the inside, you'll never get it right on the outside.

The strongest brands are built from the inside out. The brand simply reflects the culture of the organization in a focused way.

Once, when I presented a positioning strategy to a senior manager of a client company, he clearly felt let down. "Where's the magic?" he asked. "This simply describes the way we are on our best day." That's when I told him that I thought his words were the best description of brand positioning and strategy I'd heard in a long time. Suddenly, we both had a better understanding of brand strategy.

So let me state the point more formally:

Your brand position distills, focuses and bottles the essence of who and what you can be on your very best day.

Great brand strategies are inspirational. Great brand strategies are aspirational. But they must be real to the people in the know—the organization itself. The organization must believe that the strategy's inherent promise to the customer can be met. Brand strategies can represent a stretch goal, but if they don't seem real and within reach, it's just more boardroom and marketing department pipe dreaming to the rest of the organization.

After that senior manager and I nailed down what we felt was the optimal brand strategy for the company, several people in the organization identified a critical roadblock to delivering that strategy. This turned out to be a catalyzing event, as the CEO promptly took the steps necessary to ensure that the customer promise inherent to the strategy could be delivered by the organization. In doing so, he took that process problem and turned it into brand and business strength.

Now let's look at an example of what happens when brand strategy goes wrong. When Sears asked customers to "Come See the Softer Side of Sears," the company created a compelling strategic offer. The strategic "aha!" behind this customer invitation was the simple but pivotal realization that women drove revenue. Even in the hardware department, more than 50 percent of purchases were made by women. In other words: get more women into the store = sell more stuff.

This catalytic idea was successfully executed via an advertising campaign from Young & Rubicam that aimed to drive more women into Sears. That's when everything went sideways. The apparel featured in the campaign was only available in a limited number of stores—and Sears' employees knew it. They also knew that the company's sales staff had been reduced to the point where the chance of these new female customers getting any on-floor assistance was slim. The sad result was that when women walked in, eager to discover the new, softer side of Sears, the vast majority simply found the same old Sears, and the outfits they had seen in the ads (and which had brought them into the store in the first place) were nowhere to be found.

The reality was that Sears' organization saw through this strategy long before the customer did. Had the strategy been executed internally first and delivered across all stores in a way that kept customers coming back, it might well have succeeded. If only.

Similarly, once United Airlines launched its "Rising" campaign, which highlighted the airline's commitment to improving customer service, flight attendants and ground staff knew the company was in trouble. The campaign quickly became the butt of jokes internally and, worse yet, was used as ammunition and as a standing joke by passengers whenever they were disappointed with service delivery. In truth, "Rising" never had the faintest chance of liftoff. In general, flight attendants for U.S. airlines today are fairly depressed about their lot in life, and it has been showing for years. Like all of us, these people want to be proud of their jobs and the brands they represent. They want to do their jobs well. But when the service experience you represent sucks this badly, it's really tough not to let your disappointment show.

To return to a successful strategy of building brand from the inside out, consider Apple. The way I imagine it, one day, years ago, a senior product development person walked into Steve Jobs' office with a prototype of the iPod. Even at that stage of development it was no doubt amazing—more elegant and better than any MP3 player on the market. Apple-worthy in many ways but not yet "perfect." So Mr. Jobs gets a bit upset, maybe he even tosses the manager out of his office. Perhaps he even shouts at the product team for "just not getting it." The team goes back to work to make it "Steve Jobs perfect," and the rest is history.

I have absolutely no idea whether or not this incident took place but, as a consumer, I *feel* that it did. I suspect that many conversations like this took place within Apple, both with and without Steve Jobs physically present. Why? Because that's the kind of culture I bought into when I bought my iPod, then my iPhone, then my....

Apple. Nike. Southwest. Virgin. Yahoo! Starbucks. Wal-Mart. Microsoft. Google. Burton. Quicksilver. MTV. Miramax. PowerBar. Clif. Red Bull. All amazing brands, and all built from the inside out.

I once ran an ad agency in Seattle, where one day I got a call from a guy named Jeff Bezos. He and his marketing head wanted to know if we were interested in doing some "branding" work for them. We walked a couple of hundred yards down the road to a small, abandoned-looking warehouse where a grand total of six employees had desks made of doors. Looking back, it's hard to do justice to the passion of this team; you had to see the fascination in their eyes (particularly Jeff's) as we looked through the various books that different people were ordering.

The sad fact is I just didn't get it. I'd had a busy day and instead of begging for a job, I walked back to my office. My loss, as they've managed to do pretty well without me.

But I wasn't so blind as to not notice the culture in that warehouse. Even with only a half-dozen people, the culture filled the place. The sense of mission. The genuine love of books and curiosity about people's relationship with them. And one man's complete and utter determination to succeed. To make a difference.

As with Amazon, many of the world's strongest brands were built by entrepreneurs or singular, determined leaders. They were built from the ground up, with a strong brand culture from the start (even if no one ever uttered the B word). The brand was built one brick at a time, always keeping in mind what the wall needed to look like as it grew. Brand building is tough work, which is why so few start-ups succeed. It takes such strong and determined leadership that most of us are simply not up to the challenge.

(By the way, why do we brand observers never talk about the Trump brand? Love him or hate him, Donald Trump gets positioning, probably even more than he gets real estate. He's unapologetic. Unafraid to polarize. He's a man on a mission—an incredibly savvy marketer and totally committed brand marketer. And how about those Kardashians? Amazing bunch of incredibly determined brand builders. It's scary!)

Unlike a founder with a vision, the brand marketer generally inherits a brand and therefore needs to study that brand and the culture that supports it. This may seem easier than pioneering a brand, but in many ways it's actually more difficult. For one thing, you must be ruthlessly honest about the internal culture and its capabilities, as well as the strategies that the organization can and will rally behind. Listen to the organization and the brand and they will tell you what to do. Understand the brand deeply and it will show you how to grow your business. (And, sometimes more important, how not to.)

When Reebok challenged Nike based upon the growth of a new activity called aerobics, Nike stopped listening to its brand. Instead, it defended its business by following Reebok. That is, Nike got into aerobics. By definition, it softened its style.

Now, keep in mind: Nike is not a defender or a follower brand. Nike isn't all white and soft. Nike believes that the best defense is a good offense. Nike likes to kick ass.

Once Nike realized what it was doing—and went back to listening to the brand—it went on the offensive. It dubbed Reebok a poseur—i.e., a shoe company for "lightweights." The company's message became: If you are serious about sport, Nike is your brand. If you want to dance, buy Reebok. It was back to basics. Back to brand truth. Nike never looked back, and has consistently expanded its business and brand attitude across product categories, age groups and the sexes, though always in a way that is true to a very demanding culture and a very demanding brand.

But what do you do when you need to introduce a new brand strategy into an existing organization? It's not so easy, especially if you want to do it right. How do you avoid the skeptical (and typical) organizational response that the strategy you've spent so much time developing is merely the latest in a long line of marketing initiatives?

Obviously, the best starting point is to have the right strategy. One that seems real. Not only must the strategy be more than right analytically, it also must *feel* right to people who know. It must be emotionally compelling. And it must seem to have arisen from the culture itself—even as it focuses and drives that culture.

The right brand strategy screams competitive advantage. There may be many places where a company's internal culture meets the needs of the external customer, but there are few that actually yield competitive advantage. Unfortunately, the customer can't tell you which ones they are. It's your job to find the best of those few.

Let's assume you've found that right strategy, that optimal brand position. What next?

First, you need to recruit your senior management team. This team must become serious brand advocates or failure is all but assured. Most of all, your CEO must become the brand champion. If the CEO cannot champion the brand in a convincing and real way, you're sunk. If he or she cannot channel the brand in a natural way, someone has a lot of work to do.

Don't worry: most serious marketing organizations do this part of the process pretty well.

That said, you still shouldn't take the recruiting of your senior management team for granted, particularly as you transition from one CEO and leadership team to the next. For example, Wal-Mart went from strength to strength under a successful management team for twenty years after the passing of Mr. Sam. Nonetheless, as we've seen over the last few years, it has remained an ongoing challenge for the company's management team to channel the Wal-Mart brand as effectively as this retailing legend did.

The second step is to "operationalize" your strategy. That is, you need to bring the strategy to life in activities that your employees actually do every day. Ask yourself the following questions:

- How does the strategy drive product development and design?

- What about engineering?

- How does the strategy impact the office environment?

- How is the strategy "sold" by the sales force?

- How can HR use the strategy to help hire the right people?

Unlike the first step, not as many organizations handle this second course of action well.

Third, you need to "launch" your strategy to your organization, typically through some combination of a company-wide meeting, departmental presentations, and internal marketing vehicles such as the company's Intranet, brand books, screensavers, etc. But you also need to think past the launch as a solitary event, and instead begin thinking about an ongoing media plan that targets the organization just as your external media plan targets customers. Don't forget: in many cases the customer will get a greater sense of the brand from personal contact with the organization than from mass communications.

Think of it as leading a psychologically healthy cult. Cut out the isolation and chanting, but keep the consistency and repetition. Give your organization a sense of mission. Clearly demonstrate through your own actions that your common mission will be zealously pursued and that off-mission activities, no matter how tempting, will be resisted. Watch for opportunities to more dramatically prove that you're deadly serious about your mission. And watch for any possible inconsistency—it'll kill you.

Take your time. Sell the strategy internally. Build organizational understanding and support. Make the strategy and the brand position a cultural focus inside the organization before using them in the outside world. Put simply: make it real inside if you want any shot at making it real outside.

5

Want a Great Brand?
Build a Great Product.

You can only sell sizzle for so long. Sooner or later a person's got to sit down and eat.

O ver the course of a year, strategists from Sterling Brands conduct face-to-face interviews with some ten thousand people about brands. In one study in 2005, Sterling talked to teens across the country about which brands they felt were the "coolest." Actually, the team introduced them as brands, but the teens consistently responded by calling them products. Keep in mind, these teens are some of the smartest consumers to ever walk this planet. They totally understood the concept of brand, but they invariably started with the quality of the product or service.

For example, the Sterling team talked to these teens about Microsoft. Now, if you're an adult, that particular brand carries baggage. Back the '90s, Microsoft was perceived as a bully. It cast FUD (fear, uncertainty and doubt) over the competition, then showed up late with a product in need of improvement. But to teens, Microsoft was about success, ubiquity and utility. For them, Microsoft worked, and it worked well; after all, it made their lives easier. To them—at least early in the new millennium—Microsoft was almost as cool a brand as Apple, but for wildly different reasons.

Then along came the iPod and the iPhone. We've literally stopped asking young people questions about which brands are most cool or "get you the most." The answer is almost always the same: Apple. It gets boring after a while.

Sterling strategists also talked to teens about buying games. In one instance, they asked a boy what might influence him to buy a specific game once he was in the store. The response was, essentially: "You'd have to be an idiot, or an adult, to make your mind up in the store." Pressed for more detail, the teen explained: "You go online and read reviews, look at a demo, email or IM your friends and then borrow the game if you can. If you can't, you rent it. Then (and only then) do you put $50 in your pocket and go to the store."

This chapter could also be called "U is for Utility." Today's customer, particularly the younger one, is all about utility. What can it do for me and at what price? Value has always been an implied and personal equation of utility over price. The difference is that today's information technology makes the equation so much more transparent. Indeed, mobile apps are rapidly transforming information into a new form of entertainment.

With information ubiquitous and accessible from a variety of personal devices, your utility coefficient had better be higher than that of your competitors. Either that or you'd better have the infrastructure essential to support a lower price. You need to pick one road or the other, because information acts to take the middle road away.

To place this in perspective, one study found that just 4 percent of people said they would "stick with a brand if its competitors offered better value at the same price." Maybe this percentage has always been really low (though I'll bet it has dropped dramatically in recent years). But the scary fact is that soon, whether using their computer at home or their cell phone while standing in the store aisle, customers will know the exact price (and utility) difference.

This is critically important, as I still hear people wanting to talk about brand equity or brand essence, as if it's this free-floating construct. Any conversation that isolates the brand, separating it from product or service utility, ignores the realities of the marketplace—and thus risks a tragic outcome.

6

A Brand is a Response, Not a Stimulus.

Yes, I've made this point before, but as we marketers are great believers in repetition, I intend to keep at it.

A brand is a collective marketplace response, hopefully to the stimulus of a well orchestrated, focused and attention-getting marketing program. When you develop a compelling position and an associated strategy, you have gone a long way toward establishing the response that you'd like to elicit from your audience. *But you still have to craft the stimulus.*

And the stimulus doesn't work in a vacuum, either. Rather, the stimulus operates in the medium of the customer's mind, and that medium is in turn impacted by everything from the customer's long and deeply held beliefs to what he or she had for breakfast an hour ago . . . so you'd better know them both intimately before you start constructing that stimulus. More on this later, but for now, to know your customers' beliefs intimately means to know them personally. There's nothing wrong with that big, quantitative U&A study or with customer segmentation research, but there's no substitute for personally mixing it up with a few real live customers and prospects.

Once again: You don't build a brand—your audience does. You don't give a brand to the marketplace—you *get* a brand from the marketplace. Until the marketplace says you have a brand, you simply have a product. And there's nothing wrong with having a great product or service. Just don't mistake it for a great brand.

SECTION 2

POSITION IS AN
EIGHT-LETTER WORD

7

Differentiation— Often Discussed, Seldom Achieved

Strong products and services are highly differentiated from all other products and services.

It's that simple. It's that difficult.

Never has a sentence about marketing received more head nods and less true understanding than the sentence that opens this chapter. It's a statement that has always been an accepted part of marketing lore, and one that became fact when Young & Rubicam actually spent the money, built their "Brand Asset Valuator" and proved it.

Relevant differentiation was found to be a leading indicator. (Any idiot can be different. The tricky part is to be different in a way that is relevant to your audience.) Traditional measures such as knowledge and esteem were found to be lagging indicators. These lagging indicators (the ones we seem to spend so much time and money tracking) degrade slowly and can be artificially maintained through marketing expenditure or price discounting. Thus, by the time they start to fall off, you might already be in a ton of trouble.

I've always found it fascinating that the consumer packaged goods industry is so full of B-word job titles: Brand Directors, Brand Managers, Brand Assistants, etc. At the end of each year a lot of very smart brand people get their report cards. Revenues, cases, market share, profitability, distribution—the list is long and comprehensive. But the most important measures are usually nowhere to be found: Is your product or service differentiated in a way that is *meaningful* to your audience? And did that difference increase or decrease?

In most companies, astonishingly, differentiation isn't even tracked. Keep in mind, the people behind all this are brilliant people; some are the superstars of the marketing and management world. Certainly they are smart enough to know that important things get measured—and that those things that are measured tend to show up in their evaluations and determine their bonuses. So if difference isn't measured and case volume is, guess which one gets priority whenever they come into conflict (such as at the end of the accounting year)? "You'll weaken your brand position" almost always loses out to "If I don't provide a deep discount and launch that line extension I won't make my volume forecast."

Brands are built by intelligent and creative marketing. Marketing is all about positioning. Positioning is all about differentiation. Track that differentiation and you're able to track the creation and evolution of your brand. But don't stop there. You should also track specific outcomes. For example, track the premium that people are willing to pay for your product over a generic product, and use the resulting data as a proxy for brand strength. Find an appropriate way, any appropriate way, to measure brand strength and use it—along with all the other business measures. An accurate and trended measure of differentiation can be a great tool (see Y&R about their Brand Asset Valuator), but simple measurement and accountability count most in the end.

When I was at Kellogg's (pre-Brand Asset Valuator, and so long ago it hurts), we simply measured the value of our brands by comparing them to house brand equivalents. The difference in perceived value was measured once a year and then tracked. We were less interested in the absolute difference than we were in the trend. An upward trend meant good brand stewardship, while a downward trend meant poor brand stewardship and the need for intervention.

It really is that simple.

8

Difference Must Be More Than Skin Deep

I t's not enough to differentiate yourself or even to become eccentric. That perspective must also be incorporated into your strategy. You need to build a differentiated *business proposition.*

Differentiation or eccentricity—you can't just paste it onto your business with the glue of marketing communication. It needs to be solidly baked into the business. It needs to be real.

Let me pause here for a second. As much as I love absolutes, I need to back away from that statement. You actually *can* paste difference on through marketing. Two of my favorite examples are Axe and Dove—both of which are highly successful businesses that exist within Unilever. Neither business has a truly differentiated product but both have built their brands around highly differentiating points of view. Without a doubt, they'd both be in better, more defensible positions with more differentiated products, but both have done a pretty remarkable job of positioning. Both brands have been eccentric and provocative, but entirely through their points of view and some great marketing execution.

Eccentric leaders dream of creating truly different businesses. But marketing can only do so much. If you can't start with a truly differentiated business concept, you're looking at the marketing equivalent of playing with one hand tied behind your back. It's possible, but it's not the recommended path to success. This is particularly true today, as a technology-enabled marketplace simply doesn't leave much room for the weak and undifferentiated ideas that might have carved out a successful existence among the inefficiencies and geographical soft spots of the old economy.

Microsoft today represents one of the most powerful business propositions ever: every personal computer needs an operating system, so let's own that OS. But think of a young Bill Gates, who dropped out of Harvard in the early and very uncertain days of the PC industry. He developed a product and IBM offered him millions of dollars to buy it. I'm not ashamed to admit that I would've taken the money and run. But not Bill Gates; he risked throwing the whole deal away by demanding that Big Blue award him an unheard-of licensing arrangement. Different. Eccentric. But also determined and brave—and definitely not crazy.

These days Microsoft faces a very real threat in Google, which is driven by two new and equally eccentric entrepreneurs, Larry Page and Sergey Brin. Imagine the sheer audacity behind a mission to "organize the world's information." Imagine building a huge global business around an idea as deceptively simple as "search." While everyone else was busy figuring out how to hang onto visitors—that is, how to become "sticky"—Google went in the opposite direction. It focused on making its transactions so efficient that the user would spend the absolute minimum amount of time on Google's site. Page and Brin's eccentricity was their belief that we would keep coming back, again and again, thereby building search into the Web's strongest organizing principle. Google's brilliance was in finding a way to turn all those visits into profits.

Page and Brin weren't thinking of building a brand when they started out. Like other entrepreneurs before and since, they dreamed of making a difference—and of making a lot of money in the process. They were driven, focused and, most important, different. They didn't think about being different, they just were. They started with a differentiated business concept, around which they built incredibly strong organizational cultures, one person at a time. Given the low odds of success, if you didn't share the dream, you didn't join the company. The founders weren't afraid to be different. And they weren't in the least bit concerned with being considered eccentric.

They were people are on a mission. You may not have liked what they stood for, but you damn well knew what it was.

I once read an interview with Steve Jobs, who was the ultimate business phoenix. What struck me most about this particular interview was that Jobs made it very clear that Apple leadership knew it was making company-size-limiting decisions when it stuck with its proprietary hardware/software system. The managers understood the repercussions but they did it anyway. Why? Because they thought the alternative was "lame." This is the kind of attitude that builds great brands. Okay, so it can also be the attitude that leads to spectacular business failure, but you have to respect it and recognize its potential.

Consider Whole Foods, another very interesting, highly differentiated idea amidst a sea of sameness. John Mackey, the co-founder and CEO, is clearly a different kind of guy who runs a different kind of company. While organic is what Whole Foods sells, organic is also what it is. Stores are "eco-powered" and the whole in-store experience is organic. The CEO's salary is capped at no more than fourteen times the average worker's pay and employees can look at one other's salaries. Employees actually like to work there, a major reason why customers like to shop there.

I've always been a fan of Whole Foods but recently I read an old piece that illustrated just how seriously this company and its leader took their mission. After being chastised by an animal rights activist at a shareholder meeting, Mackey offered up his email address and initiated a few weeks of digital correspondence that failed to convince either party. Mackey then read several books on animal rights, decided that he was wrong, and sent another email asking the activist to help him rewrite Whole Foods' animal welfare policy.

That's a different kind of person. Whole Foods is a different kind of company.

These are people of no small ambition. These are people of vision who have the ability to inspire others. The best of them inspire everyone, from the top of their company to the bottom. Consider John F. Kennedy and his declaration that "We will go to the moon." He then fully committed his "company" to a new, different and incredibly ambitious goal. Bill Gates very early on stated a goal of "a computer on every desktop." Jeff Bezos was always sure that he was building the world's biggest bookstore, even when he was one of six people sitting in a tiny warehouse with empty shelves. (Remember, I'm the idiot who visited him and left without asking for a job.) Google wanted to "organize the world's information." Henry Ford committed himself to making a $250 car that every American could afford. As Jerry Porras and Jim Collins pointed out so well in their 1994 book, *Built to Last: Successful Habits of Visionary Companies,* great companies are built around "big, hairy, audacious goals."

Marketing is important, but the difference between making the best out of an undifferentiated idea and taking absolute advantage of a truly differentiated business proposition is so vast it almost defies measure. Never believe that smart, creative marketing can substitute for a flawed or non-differentiated business proposition. And never, ever underestimate the cultural, business and brand building power of a visionary.

> *Life's battles don't always go to the stronger or faster man,*
> *But sooner or later the man who wins*
> *Is the one who thinks he can.*

Mind you, as much as I like the sentiment expressed in the quotation above (which has been variously attributed to Napoleon Hill and Vince Lombardi, among others), I have to mention that a friend of mine recently countered it with another timely quote, this one from the early-twentieth-century writer Damon Runyon:

The battle does not always go to the strong, nor the race to the swift, but that is the way to bet.

9

Eccentricity Rules

This chapter is my call for a more extreme approach to differentiation. In today's volatile, global economy it is no longer enough to be different. You now need to be eccentric.

The dictionary defines eccentric as:

Departing from a recognized, conventional or established norm.

Many of our favorite brands are eccentric. Not surprisingly, their eccentricity often grows out of the fact that many were built by determined and equally eccentric entrepreneurs. Richard Branson of Virgin. Herb Kelleher of Southwest. Howard Schultz of Starbucks. Phil Knight of Nike. Jeff Bezos of Amazon. Charles Schwab. Jerry Yang and David Filo of Yahoo! (the early years). Sergey Brin and Larry Page of Google. Steve Jobs of Apple and Pixar. Mark Zuckerberg of Facebook. Sam Walton of Wal-Mart. The Weinstein brothers of Miramax (and now their own Weinstein Company). Jake Burton of Burton Snowboards. Ben and Jerry of ice cream fame.

We need to go to school on these people.

These people were (and in many cases still are) eccentric, but they're also leaders in the best sense of the word. Perhaps they weren't always the best managers, but let's not confuse management with leadership. And let's not confuse planning with vision.

Each of their businesses had more than a clear position; it also had a strong and heartfelt point of view. A point of view considered downright eccentric by some. In addition, the people who worked for these leaders had a real passion for what they were creating. They had a sense of mission for which they were willing to make enormous sacrifices.

As customers, we picked up on the missions. We joined the movements and we felt a sense of ownership—and we happily urged our friends to join us.

These leaders had an elemental need to build something different. They started something different, hired like-minded people to help them, and then stuck around to ensure that what they built remained different. We also know from their biographies that each of these leaders (as well as others like them) were told in no uncertain terms by people supposedly more expert than they that the thing they wanted to build could not be built. They listened and then they did it anyway. "Doing it anyway" is eccentric.

One of the reasons this list isn't long is that most who follow this path actually fail, so it's definitely not for the faint of heart. But the few who succeed become famous—and very rich. Let's face it: most of us lack the nerve and sheer willpower to be one of these people. But we can learn from them—particularly when it comes to marketing.

In many ways, things are so much harder for entrepreneurs. They've invested their own money—and certainly their own sweat. Their passion is on the line. They are all in. In other ways, however, professional marketers have the more difficult job. They don't have the luxury of starting with a small group of people who are committed to their vision. Instead, they must convince an entire organization to do something that no one else is doing. Even if they aspire to eccentric difference, there are no role models, case studies or track records. They may not even be able to "prove" their points of view, because truly differentiated positions, while built upon logic and analysis, almost always require an intuitive leap of some kind.

True differentiation is, by definition, a lonely road.

Truly great marketing involves true eccentricity. As such, it's not a game for the faint of heart. You don't just have to dare yourself to be different. You have to dare the *entire company* to be different. You must have the presence of a buttoned-down businessperson but the heart of a radical. Since you are playing with the house's money, you may sleep better at night than any entrepreneur. But entrepreneurs can have "successful" failures. In the eyes of most boards and executive teams, you cannot.

10

Differentiated Advantage

Without a doubt, it all starts with difference—but there are many ways to be different. In fact, any idiot can be different. The trick is to be different in a way that is highly relevant to your audience. Different in a way that creates competitive advantage. Advantage that is, over time, as sustainable as possible.

All of which is to say—it's not easy.

You're playing the game to win. To win, you need to be better than everyone else who is also playing to win. Generally, we marketers get this fact. We're very prepared to play to win, but we're not so prepared to be truly different. Why?

Let's blame the system. Most of us grew up with similar names, dressed in similar clothes, went to similar schools. We "manage" our differences lest our peers find us strange. We make fun of the odd ones. We fit in. This is why most of our highly differentiated brands were created by oddball entrepreneurs. They grew up different. They thought different. They were different. And therefore they created highly differentiated products and services.

But I digress. This is about advantage as much as it is about difference.

Difference + Advantage = Differentiated Advantage.

If you look at Batman, he's different because he actually went out and built his own powers. He's a self-made superhero. But does anyone care? Turns out that kids do, in fact, care. As a result, the Batman brand can position itself through differentiated advantage.

Apple is different because of its elegant design fusion of software and hardware. Bill Gates didn't think people would care enough about this to overcome a superior business model. He saw it as a profound disadvantage, in fact, and he was almost completely correct—but Steve Jobs took that "almost" and ran with it. More recently, some have questioned whether, in a cloud-based content world, anyone would care about elegantly designed devices. But play with an iPad, then with a Kindle Fire—you'll care. Apple is different. Apple is better. Apple has differentiated advantage.

It's great that Dyson carpet cleaners (and now heaters) are different, but they are designed in a way that is both different and better. It's nice that Virgin Airlines wanted to create a unique flying experience, but it succeeded because that experience was markedly better than that offered by traditional airlines. Hybrids were clearly a different kind of car, but until Prius designed a better kind of car, that difference was without meaning.

In the eyes of your customers, better but not different can still win the race, but it'll be a hard-fought race every inch of the way. Different in a way that your customers don't perceive as better won't take you very far.

Difference + Advantage = Differentiated Advantage = Great Positioning.

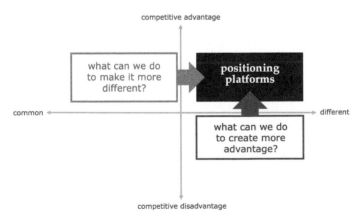

11

The Importance of the Missionary Position

[Although this chapter is primarily for single or master-branded companies, and less for portfolio companies such as packaged goods firms, I like to think that it has something for everyone.]

True differentiation runs deep.

In some companies, the product is seen as the visible reflection of the culture—and, as customers, we sense it.

What we think of as the brand often seems more like a simple lens through which we can experience the tightly focused culture behind it. As customers, we don't think this cultural connection through very deeply; we just kind of feel it and sense it to be true. Thus, when we sense a culture that we identify with, we also sense a brand we can identify with (and the other way around).

We sense a product or service we want to participate in, not simply buy.

Most important, when we actually do come into contact with this type of culture, the uniqueness and strength of the brand is tangible. You can breathe it; you can almost touch it.

A case in point: You don't have to like the people at Nike, but you sure as hell know that they're a competitive group of individuals. It's a huge company now, but that competitive edge is still in the air in Beaverton, Ore. It's in the water. It's embedded, and company employees stopped apologizing for it a long time ago. You might not like the fact that CEO Phil Knight referred to Olympic silver as "losing gold" but you certainly appreciate that he is a competitive character.

By the same token, although you may not like the Southwest travel experience, you can't help but be impressed by it. You expect a low cost, efficient airline and Southwest's sheer efficiency is what brings you back as a customer. The fact that Southwest employees seem both committed and happy is icing on the cake. It may not look that difficult to pull off, but consider JetBlue's bumpy ride to build a viable competitor to Southwest.

And if you've read any background on Steve Jobs and his team, it's pretty obvious that Jobs rejected many solutions that others would have settled for as they strove to create the "perfect" iPod, iPhone and iPad. The uncompromising perfection of the design suggests a culture you have to admire—as well as an aesthetic you want to be a part of. And every time you come into contact with the Apple culture—from its advertising to its stores to its products, and even to its logo—that aesthetic is reinforced and made more true to you.

In other words, great brands are built on the inside before being discovered by an outside culture that shares their values. Great brands have a sense of mission. They live their mission; they don't just mouth the words. When you buy the product or service, you are buying into this sense of mission. You are participating with the provider, not just buying from it. These brands have true cultural uniqueness. They have developed ways to "operationalize" this cultural uniqueness and harness it as a competitive advantage in the marketplace.

Consider this manifesto from the Burton Snowboards website:

Burton Manifesto

- We stand sideways.
- We sleep on floors in cramped resort hotel rooms.
- We get up early and go to sleep late.
- We've been mocked.
- We've been turned away from resorts that won't have us.
- We are relentless.
- We dream it, we make it, we break it, we fix it.
- We create.
- We destroy.
- We wreck ourselves day in and day out and yet we stomp that one trick or find that one line that keeps us coming back.
- We progress.

Think they know what they're all about? Burton is an original. As a business and as a culture, Burton is a pure celebration of difference.

Ditto for a company (and brand) by the name of Quicksilver, which is the largest sportswear company on the planet. "Quicksilver lives the lifestyle it is selling," *Sports Illustrated* reported in 2005. "If you work there, it is practically a requirement to surf, skate or snowboard." Many of the senior managers have decided against individual offices and simply hang out in the company's common space, using their BlackBerrys to stay in touch.

Quicksilver completely gets the need to stay "core" as the company gets larger. It understands the importance of balancing the natural tension between authenticity and size. Company management knows it has to keep core customers convinced that staying true to the company's roots is actually more important to them than getting bigger and more profitable.

It's easy to look at companies like Burton and Quicksilver and think they are totally unlike your company, that they are edgy, passionate businesses that operate in edgy, passionate categories. As a result, it's easy to think that your category is just not that exciting.

But that is cheating. It is your job to find the drama. Find the passion and bring it! Find a way to apply it to your category and into the very heart of your company's culture. It is your job to create and maintain a sense of mission. Granted, your job will be harder than that of your counterpart at Quicksilver, who enjoys a supportive and focused corporate culture, but you can't give up on it.

As an example, take a look at a software firm called SAS, which is consistently rated one of the best companies to work for in America. CEO Jim Goodnight, who has steadfastly refused to take his company public, despite the fact that doing so would make him incredibly rich, honestly views the SAS workforce as a family. Extensive employee services, including daycare, education and recreation, are all available at SAS's North Carolina campus. The great thing about Goodnight's paternal feelings toward his company is that they are genuine. Listen to this man talk and you want to work for him.

People who work at SAS appreciate the unique culture they belong to. And many talented people who don't work there would like to. Just as important, I think customers want to give this company their money. What that means is that all other things being equal (or even just close), SAS's culture and moral compass are what really drive its revenue. Low turnover (SAS has an industry low of less than 4 percent) and high morale also drive the company's top line—and contribute to the bottom line as well.

The same is true of Costco. Like SAS (and Starbucks), Costco is an employee-first company. Costco treats its people well: it pays them better than others in the industry and provides them with a better benefits package. Happy employees, extremely low turnover and a dynamic growing business with a very loyal customer base. Coincidence? Not on your life. A brand built from the inside out? Absolutely.

Put simply, there are no terminally dull categories or products. It's just a question of determination and imagination.

This is a vitally important point that all marketers need to get into their heads. Categories often seem dull and undifferentiated . . . to the point of being described as commodities by a majority of participants and observers. And that stays true right up to the point where some company creates a truly differentiated proposition and a passionate culture around which it can create competitive advantage and dramatic growth. Suddenly, no one is talking about a "commodity" anymore.

I've lost track of the number of times I've been told by a marketer that his or her company operates in a "commodity category." I always respond the same way: *There are no commodity categories, just commodity marketers.* (Don't get me wrong: acting as a commodity is a completely valid business strategy, though I'd argue that you'd better get the money in early as it won't last long. I would also say that this strategy has no room for a real marketer.)

Sometimes the "idea" or the "drama" is right in front of your eyes, and sometimes it may seem impossible to find. But you should always assume that it is there. Create your brand's mission. Build your brand and company culture around it. "Operationalize" it.

If it's real and if it runs deep, a culture-based competitive advantage will stand the test of time. By comparison, a product- or service-based advantage, while also critical to success, will prove more transitory.

I know, I know. That's easy to say and hard to do. But at least give it a shot.

12

Don't Be a Prisoner

It's easy to become a prisoner of your point of view.

Two very smart people from two very different worlds made this crucial point in different ways. Not surprisingly, one was Steve Jobs. In a 2005 interview with *Fortune* magazine about companies that were (or weren't) on top of the move to digital music, he noted: "Some companies are prisoners of their point of view." (Typical Jobs: small statement, big point of view. That's just one reason he's already missed so much.) Ted Levitt made more or less the same point in "Marketing Myopia" a renowned *Harvard Business Review* article published in 1960. In it, Levitt argued that corporations (and sometimes entire industries) are held prisoner by how they define their market.

Early train and bus companies, for example, defined their business in terms of trains and buses rather than transportation and thus missed out on flight. Similarly, old film studios defined their business as movies instead of entertainment and missed out on television. More recently, Barnes & Noble and Borders defined their business as mere bookstores for far too long and were "Amazoned."

No doubt Jobs had an ulterior motive for his statement (didn't he always?), in that he needed consumer electronics manufacturers and others to jump on the let's-make-great-entertainment-products-that-run-off-the-iPod-brain bandwagon. But that doesn't mean he wasn't right.

Kids today find the idea of buying and carrying around plastic containers filled with CDs remarkably quaint. They also increasingly find the physical buying and renting of movies to be curious behavior. Music and movies will stay digital, and a very large industry is growing up around their storage, discovery, delivery and consumption. Companies that embrace this transformation will prosper, while those in denial will fail.

Blockbuster defined its business as "physically rented movies." Despite the sheer size of the franchise at its peak, that definition still put Blockbuster on a very short runway to oblivion. On the flip side, if MGM (the casino and entertainment MGM, not the film studio) had limited itself to gambling instead of branching out into other areas of adult entertainment, it would be a much smaller and more vulnerable business than it currently is.

So be careful. The seemingly simple act of defining the business you're in can have a profound impact on your strategy—from the business model all the way through to brand and marketing strategy. Defining your business serves to define your competitive set. Most people have a tendency to define their business, and therefore their competitive set, too tightly. They then pay the price when their business is "disrupted" by someone they didn't even consider competition.

Spend time on this most basic question and spend that time early. Don't wait for a crisis and never leave it to others to determine when you get around to addressing it. Bring in outsiders for the express purpose of torturing the logic of your market definition.

Finally, if you created an apparently successful strategy and you're still around because it's been working, task a couple of young Turks to show you why it's all wrong. I speak from experience—it's a case of losing objectivity through strategic ownership. Like it or not: if you're the author of a strategy, you can also become a prisoner of it.

Define your business, and define it carefully. But consider that definition malleable and invite others to challenge it. Listen carefully. Then create an organizational environment where people are rewarded for challenging the status quo. If someone successfully challenges your status quo before an unseen competitor does, he or she may well save the company.

13

Invent, Don't Construct

Analysis is great, but creating true differentiation is essentially a leap of faith.

Differentiation is seldom achieved purely through analytical rigor. Analysis and incrementalism still have their place in business, just not in the actual creation of differentiation.

The answer is to *know everything*. Strive to be more analytically rigorous than your competitors but also assume they're looking at the same data and probably arriving at very similar conclusions. As heard in the movie *The Incredibles*: "When everyone is super, no one is."

So go ahead and build that mountain of information. After that, climb to the summit and look around. Then leap off. Use science to get you to the top, art to guide your leap.

> That which is static and repetitive is boring.
> That which is dynamic and random is confusing.
> In between lies art.
>
> *John Locke*

Two well-known books by Malcolm Gladwell (*Blink*) and Michael LeGault (*Think! Why Crucial Decisions Can't Be Made in the Blink of an Eye*) illustrate this point: you need to think before you blink. You are suicidal if you don't use every ounce of analytical rigor you have to solve your strategic problem, but you're delusional if you think that analytical exploration is sufficient for business success. Conversely, anyone who tries to build a business on a "golden gut," without taking the time to explore actual market data, is a fool.

Information is critical but it's also ubiquitous. Analysis is a given. True brand differentiation and sustainable advantage can only be found and created in one place: your imagination.

Another weakness of using analysis alone is that it tends to lead you toward so-called red oceans (red because of all the competitive blood being spilled). In other words, when you are led by things you can measure, you tend toward spaces that can be measured—and those spaces are inevitably already overbuilt. Such spaces are almost always red oceans. Blue oceans, on the other hand, are not well measured, and no amount of pure analysis will lead you to them. (Read *Blue Ocean Strategy* by W. Chan Kim and Renee Mauborgne for more information in this vein.)

Blue oceans are the lonely roads I mentioned at the beginning of the book.

This all sounds good, maybe even a bit inspiring. But as stated before, most marketers operate within large organizations and those organizations aren't known for following the intuitive leaps of their marketers. Once you've made that leap you need to put your analytical hat back on and construct the bridge from the top of that information mountain to wherever you landed. Sorry, but that's the way it works: to justify your recommended strategy, you will be asked to compare your intended path to the paths taken by others—even though the only really successful path will be the one that takes a completely different route (and thus can't be measured).

To reiterate: analyze the hell out of the situation, make your intuitive leap, and then find the analytical path that connects your landing spot back to wherever you jumped from.

Finally, if you can't handle paradoxes you may want to stay out of marketing.

14

Love Me or Hate Me—Just Don't Like Me

Positions polarize.

What you don't do and what you're willing to give up is often more important than what you do and keep. Don't be afraid. The better you are at creating a strong, clear brand position, the more likely you are to find a group of people who really don't like you. As Bill Cosby once said, "I don't know the key to success, but the key to failure is trying to please everybody."

The And1 website used to feature an extreme example of this point. Addressing the meaning behind its name, the basketball apparel company announced: "If you don't know what it means, we don't want you wearing our shoes."

It's like life: the only way to have everyone like you is to avoid taking a controversial stance on *anything*. If you are willing to be anything to anybody—to surrender your identity and your individuality—no one will have strong feelings about you either way. You won't stand out to anyone and you won't offend anyone. You simply won't matter. Is that the fate you want?

In business, a dull existence means a weak brand. If you want some people to love you, you've got to accept that others may hate you. With your company clamoring for new customers and more business, it takes a certain amount of nerve to deliberately ignore people that many within your organization might consider prospects.

After an American took second place in the Olympics, Nike CEO Phil Knight was quoted as saying, "He didn't win the silver, he lost the gold." Polarizing? You bet. Clear positioning? Hell yes! Nike is unabashedly a culture built around winning, and if you can't take the heat you have no business in that kitchen. Maybe it wasn't the most sensitive thing to say. Perhaps Mr. Knight would like a do-over on that quote. But more likely not.

Can you find fault with this kind of corporate culture? Definitely. Is this a culture for everyone? Definitely not. Do you know exactly where this company and brand stand? Most emphatically *yes*.

Las Vegas is a case study in how not to do it, followed by an even better case study in how to get it right. Several years ago the Las Vegas brain trust went into denial. It decided that Las Vegas had grown up and was ready for its debut as a family entertainment center. The people behind the new campaign were moderately successful in this endeavor—there certainly is lots of entertainment there for kids—but ultimately realized that the profit margins were to be found in adult activities. They were right to see the potential of great hotels, themed experiences and high dining, but they were wrong to think that this heralded a change in the Vegas brand.

Fast-forward a few years to a new campaign: "What happens in Vegas, stays in Vegas." It's a riff from an old line, but it absolutely nailed the essence of the Las Vegas brand. Vegas *is* for adults. It is now a remarkably more sophisticated product than it was, but its brand position remains the same.

Some people love Nike; others hate it.

Some people love Vegas; others hate it.

Every strong and focused brand, just like every strong and focused person, creates this love/hate dynamic.

Be true to who and what you are. Constantly evolve and improve the quality of your product. Be true to your brand and let the product work for you. If you find yourself outraged by the way Las Vegas markets itself (as you might well be) that's okay, because you are not the target audience. If you write a letter to the editor of the *Las Vegas Sun* to express your outrage, that's even better, because you are reinforcing the brand values of Las Vegas among its real audience. You are *supposed* to be outraged.

Eastern Mountain Sports (EMS) is an example of a retailer that completely lost its way. EMS started out as a genuinely hardcore outdoor retailer for genuinely hardcore outdoor types. But in an attempt to drive revenue, the thirty-seven-year-old company repositioned itself as a mainstream outdoors retailer, stocking its shelves with lots of soft, fleecy and approachable stuff. Well, no surprise: the new me-too retailing didn't drive revenue. Enter, in 2003, new CEO Jim Manzer, who described EMS at the time as a "Gap with climbing ropes."

Manzer understood positioning (though he probably never used that word) and he definitely understood the need to be different. In the years since taking over EMS, Manzer has taken the company back to its original position, beginning with restoring the hard-core outdoor culture within the company and creating a much more authentic (and therefore unique) retail experience. Polarizing? You'd better believe it.

Soccer moms in SUVs no longer shop at Eastern Mountain Sports; they're intimidated by the high-end goods and the serious-minded sales staff. But dedicated mountaineering types are back, and they feel right at home.

EMS makes me think of a new business pitch we once made to Eddie Bauer when I ran Cole & Weber. The meeting spun out of control when I began arguing with the then-head of marketing. The rest of my pitch team was appalled. We had just made (I thought) a very strong case for the unique and therefore truly differentiating characteristics of the Eddie Bauer brand. I was informed politely that I didn't really get retail, and that success could only be found in becoming more like Gap (and a couple of other, similar retailers). I responded that America already had a Gap and didn't need another one. In my mind I won the argument, but we most definitely lost the pitch. (Did you know that arguing with a potential client is not an approved new-business approach?)

And though I lost the battle, Eddie Bauer ultimately lost the war. Arguing may not work in new-business pitches, but "me-too" doesn't work in marketing.

Polarization is good. Traveling the middle road, tempting as it may be, is always and unequivocally bad. Like people, brands are defined by the company they keep. But they're also defined by the company they don't keep.

15

Position Narrow, Catch Wide

I think I first heard the above expression from Alpa Pandya, a colleague of mine at Sterling, and I'm happy to give her full credit for it.

Although obvious to the best marketers, "position narrow, catch wide" seems counterintuitive to nearly everyone else. It means that if you want to appeal to a wide audience you must position yourself in a narrow, specific way. Its corollary is that if you try to be a lot of things to a lot of people, you will be nothing to nobody. A friend read the phrase and told me about an old radio commercial that began: "Men! And that includes you girls."

Another, similar saying: "Positioning is the art of sacrifice." In other words, done right, great positioning is subtractive in nature, not additive. The road is filled with tough sacrifices you must make if you are to achieve a narrow focus.

Think of real life. The people we admire most are those who stand for something specific. They have a point of view and it's simply not negotiable. The people who get the attention of the media (for better and sometimes for worse) are also those with a strong, specific and narrow point of view.

In marketing as well as life, it takes nerve to position narrow, which is perhaps why entrepreneurs are so much more successful at it than professional brand managers. Positioning narrow entails finding your core audience, understanding it and building a sustainable relationship. Once you've done that, you can enlist that core to help the rest of the world "discover" you.

Ideally, then, you want a core audience that is inspirational to others. Nike is a great example of this. It's clear to everyone on the Nike campus and across the marketplace that Nike is a brand for the high-performance, highly competitive athlete. That said, Nike also knows that about 80 percent of its shoes are worn by people like me, often simply to go grocery shopping. Why do we buy high performance shoes if we live low-performance lives? Because we all think we have a bit of that high-performance athlete in us. And because we all feel we need to be ready and equipped to perform, even if we never do.

Nike's message? Don't confuse your core customer with your target market.

That said, *within* the organization, we first want everyone to know we are building our brand for our core customer. This is important because we want every employee to know the people for whom they are designing products, experiences and marketing. Ideally, we want everyone to have a single customer in mind. Why? Because life is so much simpler when you are designing for a solitary person instead of a faceless demographic. Ideally, we want every single employee working on the same product experience to have that same individual in mind. The long term goal, of course, is to have everyone *outside* the organization also understand the individual we are building for—and we want them to aspire to be more like that person rather than less.

Once all of this is in place, we then want to reach out to those who can best help us achieve our objectives. This might be limited to our core audience (remember the need for critical mass), but it might just as easily be directed toward those legions of still-undecided buyers.

In practice, this means our core audience is unequalled in importance. They are the people we are working for, the people for whom our brand is built. With luck, others aspire to be more like them. But that is a completely separate issue from identifying our target market when it comes to communication. In other words, *target narrow, reach wide*.

Practically speaking, you can't possibly be for everyone, so it always comes down to a matter of how targeted you can be. In most cases, however, it's more about how targeted you *have* to be given inevitable budget constraints. Even McDonald's and Wal-Mart aren't for everyone (it just seems that way), so stop sweating so much over the people who won't ever be your customers. Instead, focus on those who will.

All strong brands started with a loyal core, then build from this base. Have the patience and the confidence necessary for business building and you'll be rewarded. Snapple, Gatorade, Power Bar and SoBe are all somewhat related products. Even more, however, they are linked by the fact that tightly knit groups of people with a clear vision positioned them narrowly, then allowed them to "catch wider" as they grew. Each is now a part of much larger organizations with much larger radar screens—and their new managers need to stay sensitive and true to the point of view that got them where they are today.

When Cadillac moved to restage its brand, which was (accurately) stigmatized as being only for old folks, the first thing the company did was design a product that would appeal to younger drivers. Cadillac hit pay dirt when rap stars began snapping up the Escalade, and the marketing team quickly saw the opportunity to position the model as the prestige SUV of the hip-hop set. (The new market, while seemingly incongruous with Cadillac's modern history, fits with the company's past. Back in the 1930s the great Alfred Sloan convinced others at GM to sell to black professionals, thus saving the marque). Rappers showing off their pimped-out Escalades on MTV's *Cribs* and other venues completely changed the image of Cadillac, opening the door to the brand embarking on a massive shift toward high-performance luxury cars that continues to this day.

In what may be the whopper of all narrow product positions, Google has specialized in and come to own one simple idea: search. In the early days of Google, lots of "expert" commentators criticized this model as limited and overly specialized. But we've all now come to see what CEO Eric Schmidt knew all along: Search, by sucking away advertising dollars from every industry (all while appearing completely benign) was the killer application to end all killer applications. As we continue to expand our use of the Internet as a medium through which we live our lives, search will be the one unifying "tool" that almost all activities will pass through. If the information superhighway is the construct that makes sense to you (it shouldn't these days), think of Google as the toll collector.

If Google teaches us anything, it is to not confuse how narrowly you position your offering with the ultimate size of your business. Indeed, it's often an inverse relationship: the narrower the position, the broader the ultimate audience. Just look to Google—the narrowest and simplest of positions, and the widest of all catches.

Position narrow/target wide also applies to corporate communications. Way too much PR, advertising and point-of-sale copy is written with the belief that it is possible to convey complex information to its target audience. It almost never works. Not because the audience isn't smart enough, but because it isn't interested enough. Instead, you have to focus the message, whatever that message might be. As I used to tell clients when I worked in advertising—you can *say* whatever you want, but it's only what they *hear* that counts.

Strategy, positioning, and communication: in their best forms they are all acts of sacrifice.

16

Own Something

Don't be a player. Be an owner. Make yourself famous for something.

This may seem blindingly obvious, but you really have to do everything you possibly can to "own" something.

In the crazy early days of the Internet the keyword was space. VCs and others wanted you to define the space you would play in. Ideally, the space you would own. This was clearly a smart conversation to have. The only problem was that this space had to be big—very big. Unfortunately, this requirement resulted in start-ups chasing some amorphous, poorly defined space just so they could show investors that it was "huge." Inevitably, the space (if you could even call it that) was something the marketer could not possibly own. In addition, if that space were particularly attractive, ten other companies were chasing it just as hard.

In marketing, well-defined and ownable space beats hard-to-define non-ownable space any day of the week. You can also make the argument that those who own their space can expand that space or occupy adjacent space much more easily than can others fighting over a large piece of ill-defined real estate.

- Define your space

- Own it

- Erect barriers to block entry by others

- Expand it

Jeff Bezos decided to own the idea of online book selling back when it was a tiny, unprofitable business. He built critical mass and consolidated his ownership, building it into a very large, unprofitable business. In the same way he built the world's largest bookstore, Bezos then launched Kindle, extending the definition of books and creating an online retailer with unstoppable momentum. Along the way, he even figured out how to make money. To be fair, I don't think even Bezos saw where this would take him, and the rug could have been pulled out from under him at any time. It wasn't, however, and one smart move led to another. But it all started with *ownership*.

Yahoo! once owned search but, seduced by larger spaces, allowed Google to take that ownership away. Now Google owns search, and has successfully fought to defend it against all newcomers. Again, somewhere along the way, the company figured out how to make money—lots and lots of it.

You need to be first to own a category, a segment, a concept. If someone already beat you to it, you must then figure out how you can reinvent that category in a way that negates any previous ownership. Can you segment the category and own a new and compelling corner of it? In technology I like to compare the marketplace, with all of its analysts and influencers, competition and "coopetition," to one huge and confusing conversation. What is your part of that conversation?

Where is the area you will have the loudest voice? What is the area in which others will seek out your point of view first? Find it and own it, even if it's currently a relatively small part of the overall conversation. Make sure that analysts and the press always call you first for your point of view when it comes to this conversation. Once you've done that, only then can you begin to focus on how to move this slice of the conversation toward center stage.

On a scale that was only possible in the retail landscape of the past, this is exactly what Home Depot, Best Buy and others, the so-called category killers, did to mass merchants such as Sears and Montgomery Ward. Victoria's Secret decided to carve out an ownership position in women's lingerie. Whole Foods has taken ownership of organic food retailing. Intuit owns the idea of financial software, while Symantec has carved out a very successful business in security software.

So what are you genuinely the best at? If the answer is "nothing," you'd better like selling things really, really cheap. If you know the answer, then you should be asking yourself the following questions: Is there a real customer need that connects to and is enabled by this thing I do best? Can I bring what I'm best at to life in a way that compels the customer and creates competitive advantage?

In positioning, owning is significantly better than renting. Take your business apart and with a cold, objective eye, find the one thing you can and must own if you are to succeed.

Hone it. Build it. Expand it. Guard it with your life.

17

Niche is Not a Four-Letter Word

Wait a second. Niche is not a four-letter word but brand is? Whereas the word brand often seems like a spiritual invocation, in many marketing circles the word niche is often spoken with derision and used as a put down.

As far as niche goes, perhaps the most egregious errors of judgment were made in the technology marketplace of the late '90s, when niche became a curse you placed on any idea you wanted to kill or competitor you wanted to insult. Niche companies just weren't going to make it. Niche start-ups just weren't going to get the needed venture capital. Niches were for small-time players, the fearful, people with limited vision.

Well, I've always loved niche brands, never forgetting that bigger can indeed be better, particularly in the old economy. Needless to say, however, the Web has changed the way we think.

In 2006, *Wired* Editor Chris Anderson published *The Long Tail,* which highlighted how universal Web access meant that even the most thinly sliced niches could still add up to significant business when physical restrictions were taken out of the equation. For example, part of the dominance of big media content has always been physically derived: Limited space on a television channel or with a cable operator. Limited space on your local cinema screen, in a video rental store, in a music store or on a bookshelf. By comparison, digital distribution, universal Web access and search tools have created unlimited usable space, which has begun to make for an absolutely fascinating media marketplace that will become even more compelling in the years to come.

Seen from a different perspective, niche brands are simply brands that understand the "position narrow, catch wide" axiom we discussed earlier. They have built a limited, but fervent, following first. They own their segment—and enjoy the higher margins that generally accrue to smart niche marketers. They only break with the axiom by choosing to stay where they are. To many entrepreneurs this choice is an act of cowardice and failure. I disagree; indeed, I want to stress (even scream) that a highly profitable niche is not a bad place to stay.

Yes, it's true, businesses are, as the cliché goes, like sharks. If they don't keep moving forward they will die. But moving forward and getting big are two very different things. Who says you need to be big? A VC will if you're a start-up, which is why many of those VCs are fully responsible for killing businesses that would have survived their first downturn if they had been rigged to run in niche-mode rather than artificially scaled to run big. Once you're publicly traded, the street will demand top-line growth—until you teach your shareholders to invest in your consistent profitability rather than your explosive growth. To purely analytical financial minds, if growth is good, more growth must be better, even when the outcome might create the seeds of your long-term demise. It can be a very good strategy to break those expectations and follow your own path to long-term survival.

Owning a highly profitable niche is a thing to be celebrated. Don't make the mistake of assuming that it is a natural and evolutionary step to move out of that niche and compete on a larger and more competitive stage. For now, at least, you may be much better off staying just where you are. Also, keep in mind that several focused and successful niche plays might well offer the better path to higher revenue, higher margins and less risk exposure than one big, broad play.

If the opportunity to break out does exist, carefully plot it out. Are you going from narrow to wide, or would it be more profitable to move into a range of associated niche markets before pulling them all together?

I thoroughly enjoyed working closely with Silicon Graphics, Inc. (SGI) as it built the market for visual computing in the early '90s. As a marketer without a lot of technology experience at the time, I was perplexed as to why the term "niche" took so much abuse within the company. Suddenly, however, instead of celebrating the company's high-end visual niche (with the highest hardware margins in the business), SGI caught "scale fever," convinced that it had to double in size. Great ideas were quickly dismissed with, "that's too niche." Overnight, it became imperative that the company exploit its technological advantage in lower priced, less-mission-critical market segments.

The next thing I knew, SGI had decided to buy Cray, a company that built supercomputers so powerful and so limited in terms of customers that they were already being driven out of business by... Silicon Graphics. Why buy someone you are making irrelevant? To grow bigger and faster, of course. To avoid the stigma of being a niche player. Soon thereafter, SGI extended into smaller, cheaper machines, which was an equally crazy overextension of resources.

Large packaged goods companies offer wonderful lessons about niches. Each year entrepreneurial start-ups create niche products that, either slowly or very quickly, build a loyal and passionate following. Once they get to be "big enough," they are acquired by a much larger packaged goods company that also operates in that category—usually for a lot of money. If that very same successful idea had originally been created within the larger acquiring company, it would have been deemed too small (niche) to warrant the investment necessary to take it to market. There isn't the passion and patience required to build a niche brand, but there does seem to be the money to pay for that brand once it's a success.

You can also stretch your niche, as long as you do it intelligently. Porsche is stretching its brand permission carefully and successfully with Cayenne and Panamera. And don't forget that Apple, too, was once a niche player!

Back in my early days at Kellogg's, I had the distinct honor of working for a man named Bill LaMothe, who was chairman of the company. Unfortunately, I didn't get to work directly for him, as I was just a lowly marketing guy back then. But I once sat in a meeting and watched a manager try to sell LaMothe on the idea of getting Kellogg's into the manufacturing of private-label cereal.

He replied, categorically, that we would never do that on his watch. He believed that companies and manufacturing facilities could only accommodate one level of quality. If Kellogg's were to attempt to make both high- and low-quality cereal within the same factory, ultimately both would work their way to the middle. What would we stand for then?

LaMothe was happy to pass up a short-term opportunity to preserve the long-term health of his company. He also took a pass on a score of opportunities to diversify Kellogg's through acquisition, taking a lot of criticism from analysts until all those other consumer packaged goods (CPG) acquisitions flopped. Bill LaMothe was a visionary. He knew Kellogg's and its niche better than anyone alive, and the company is so much better today because of the revenue-limiting decisions he made along the way.

There's nothing wrong, and a lot of things right, with truly excelling at one thing.

Thinking small can actually be the best path to a big result.

18

The Joys of Disruption

Brands and brand strategies can be viewed as conceptual frameworks that demand consistency of execution. It follows then that brands promote continuity. But as stated earlier, businesses are like sharks; if they don't move forward they die. Competition disrupts continuity. So if you are not acting disruptively, odds are that a disruption will be visited upon you by someone you might not have even realized was a competitor.

The point is that you must do everything possible to be disruptive. Strategically disruptive. Disruptive at the product or service level. Disruptive at the marketing communication level. If you want my attention, you need to disrupt whatever else is holding my attention. If you want my business, you need to disrupt whatever is causing me to do business with someone else.

Remember, as already mentioned, attention has become the most precious commodity in the marketplace. Also recall how difficult it is to create real change.

There's a problem with staying in the center of the strategic "box." This kind of behavior gets an A+ for consistency but a D- for attention-getting. Tactically, your job as a marketer is to bang the hell out of the walls of that box, all while still staying inside. In other words, get creative. Make noise. Promote change. Always keep moving. Always keep building. Always stay "in-strategy." But first and foremost, always make noise.

It's a tricky business because, ultimately, you must disrupt a market-place that doesn't really want to be disrupted. Unless you love the status quo (and clear market leaders who are "on-trend" have every reason to love the status quo), you need a discontinuity to occur. The Internet has been the world's greatest discontinuity and has set the stage for dramatic upheaval in every market it touches. In other words, every market.

But generally the only way to ensure a discontinuity is to create it yourself. Whatever that discontinuity is, it must work to your advantage, and therefore must play into your brand strategy.

Napster disrupted the music market, but in a way that could never make money. Apple disrupted the music market in a way that did make money—generally a better approach.

Yahoo! disrupted the way we find information, but then acted as if it had no idea what it had done. Google knew.

In fact, when you look at the big four—Apple, Amazon, Google and Facebook—they are in the process of disrupting about a hundred different markets. You may not think you compete with these guys, but the odds are that sooner or later you will. One or the other—maybe even all— will disrupt your marketplace. Don't waste energy figuring out if this is true or not, just figure out the *how* of the disruption—then beat them to it and make it work to your advantage.

Amazon sold books, but created a disruption through the Kindle. In some ways the company even attacked its own business in order to build that business. If Amazon hadn't developed the Kindle, the book business would've been disrupted by—you guessed it—Apple. This disruption would have been terrific—as long as you work in Cupertino and not Seattle.

Today, Google owns the idea of search and Yahoo! is a minor player in that field. Now it's up to some aggressive new player to create a new discontinuity, one that works to the advantage of its brand strategy. Search is now ubiquitous—it is indeed the Internet's killer application—but therein lies both Google's opportunity and its vulnerability. Search has already started to splinter into several specialized purposes, or segments, some of which will be bigger and more profitable, some less so. Who will own entertainment search? But maybe that's too broad a question. Instead: Who will own music search? Who will own television search? Who will own local search?

In fact, you could argue that, for category leaders, letting Google dominate search behavior in your category means that you are, by definition, being disrupted by it. While I think this makes for an interesting conceptual discussion and is something marketers really need to think through, the smart money should stay with Google.

If strong specialists don't disrupt the flow, Google will own all of the segments because it now has continuity working for it. When in doubt, the marketplace turns to Google, just as the computer marketplace used to turn to IBM. Even Microsoft's strong challenge with Bing proved to be insufficiently disruptive. Microsoft attacked Google head-on instead of doing something different—something truly disruptive. Instead of saying, "We have to disrupt search," Microsoft merely said, "We'll do search better."

Unless someone creates a true disruption (for example, by successfully specializing in specific categories of search behavior)—Google will continue to control the agenda. But the reality is that the brand most likely to disrupt the search market in some way is Google itself. Why? Because Google is really good at it. And because disruption is hardwired into its DNA.

19

The Disposable Strategy

Change happens.

There's one characteristic about change that no one can deny: it happens. As a result, there is an inherent tension in establishing a clear and well-defined strategy. On the one hand, strategy needs to be sustainable, long term, and relentlessly and consistently pursued. On the other hand, time and circumstance change everything—and that includes strategy. In other words, you must design for permanence, all the while knowing it will never occur.

A brand strategy is built around a position that is held consistently over time. It follows that one position held over time (i.e., a brand) is also a more profitable strategy. Unfortunately, the pace and flux of the modern, technology-driven global economy conspire against this approach. We marketers need to be realists. Change is in the air. Choice is rampant. Competition is more intense than ever. Consistency may not be the best option. It may not even be an option.

So how do we resolve this dilemma? By stepping back and taking a broader view. A brand strategy (that is, a position held over time) is like a straight line between two points—clearly the easiest, and most profitable, path available. It is also the path with the lowest possible risk of getting lost along the way. But today that straight path may not be available. Or it may not stay open long enough for you to traverse it.

As a result, you may have to switch to the second-best strategy, which is to try to reach the same destination via a series of shorter trips—each planned out much closer to the actual departure date and each, therefore, as fully informed as possible.

An ad agency I once ran created an ad for the then-hot workstation-maker Silicon Graphics. I'll never forget the underlying concept: SGI argued that its technology allowed a company to make decisions as late in the process as possible and still get the results (typically a new product) to the marketplace in a timely manner. SGI's point was that the closer in time any decision is to its execution, the more informed, and therefore better, that decision would be.

Surely the same principle holds in marketing.

Think about this as you create a brand or marketing strategy. It should, of course, look sustainable, but it should also be adaptive—i.e., flexible enough to allow for executional change over time.

But what if a strategy is the marketing equivalent of painting yourself into a corner? What if it's neither sustainable nor adaptable?

Is that strategy, by definition, wrong? Not necessarily. Sometimes the best course of action is to embrace one strategy for a few years, then dispose of it and move on. The trick is to know that you're painting yourself into a corner and to know precisely how and when you will exit that corner.

I hate to pick on Charles Schwab, as I'm fairly certain I would have made the same mistakes, but the brand helps to illustrate my point. In the late '90s, Schwab was working from what should have been a disposable strategy designed to take complete advantage of the Internet revolution and the consequent stock market explosion. But the company, incredibly successful on the way up, shockingly had no viable strategy for the way down.

You might argue that Schwab, in fact, needed three marketing strategies. One strategy to maximize revenue in an up market, one to steal market share in a down market, and one to make the most of the period in between. Surely the company realized that it wouldn't remain the lowest cost provider as soon as it saw this thing called the Internet? Surely it realized it needed an alternative strategy?

Indeed, a series of disposable strategies may be the optimal course of action. As long as you act deliberately, you can ensure that the cost of disposing with one strategy and moving on to the next is not prohibitive. By comparison, when you create a high level of fairly fixed cost behind a strategy, you'd better be highly confident (not to mention right) about its success and staying power. "We can't change course now" is a very scary statement to hear from anyone's lips, particularly in this day and age.

An important corollary to this point of view is that you must also consider the disposal cost of your strategy, as well as the disposal cost of any kind of long-term initiative under consideration. If the world changes (and it will) or competitors undermine your strategy (and they will), is your strategy adaptive enough to meet the emerging threat or the newly visible opportunity? If not, what will it cost you to change course?

Assume change will happen. Assume that the thing that will really make the difference is how prepared you are for that change.

See? It's simple. Expect the unexpected and always keep your eye on the things you cannot see.

20

Positioning Happens

Put simply, positioning is a mandatory activity. Positioning happens whether you're actively involved in the process or not. Customers, partners, the press, analysts, word of mouth—together they conspire to create a position in the minds of your audience.

In the worst-case scenario, your competitors, sensing a vacuum, are only too happy to position your business for you. Sometimes these default positions are pretty tight and focused, and very tough to shift. Sometimes they are vague and amorphous—which may sound a little better, but really isn't.

As I mentioned earlier, I worked closely with Silicon Graphics in the halcyon days of the early 1990s. While much of its later misfortune was due, in my opinion, to market forces beyond the company's control, the marketing guy in me still bemoans SGI's lost positioning opportunity. Because SGI never forcefully positioned itself in the marketplace, that job was done for it by others: by Hollywood, as directors and producers lined up to use the company's visual computing power, and by financial and industry analysts, most of whom wanted an assurance of continued meteoric growth. Perhaps most destructively, SGI was very aggressively de-positioned by more battle-hardened competitors such as Sun Microsystems.

The result was that, by default and through the work of clever competitors, SGI became known as the maker of "computers for Hollywood and others who don't care about cost," a market too small to support SGI's growth ambitions. And so the company, once the hottest firm in the computer industry, slid into oblivion.

I think professional marketers generally get this point. But if you are a non-marketer, please understand that positioning is not an optional activity, no matter what the size of your company. If you hope to subsist on more than customers who just happened to trip over your product or service, you need to position that product or service actively. Then you need to manage that position *aggressively*.

What that means is that you must do the thinking required to create a differentiated and compelling position. Then you must develop a strategy to deliver and solidify that position with your audience. Positioning has nothing to do with advertising and nothing to do with the size of your marketing budget. Rather, it's as simple as deciding that you'll be the master of your own business destiny.

As the saying goes, if you don't know where you're going, any road will take you there. Or to use another of my favorite adages: Having lost sight of our objectives we redoubled our efforts. You need to know the position or place you're trying to occupy. The better you know it, the easier it will be to focus your efforts on getting there.

21

Find Your Difference

nyone who has anything to do with brands can tell you that they are built by being different in a way that is relevant and compelling to a particular audience. Difference is the key to the brand door. Most decent marketers get this, and most can make the case for differentiation. Yet sadly and inexplicably, very few of us actually live by these words.

Again, this is why you have to love those crazy entrepreneurs—those single-minded, completely obsessed nuts who built highly differentiated businesses through and around their ideas and sheer will. Jobs. Branson. Ellison. Bezos. And all their brethren.

Mozart once said: "I have never made the slightest effort to do anything original." Like those famous brand-building entrepreneurs, he didn't need to try to be different, he just was. But most professional marketers inherit brands and spend most of their time managing businesses; they're not starting from scratch. Most of us need to try harder to be different than did Wolfgang Mozart.

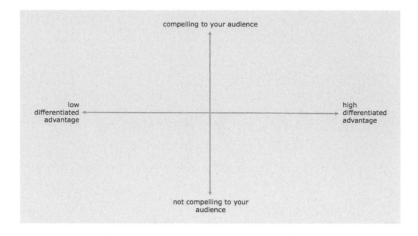

Here's a simple exercise to apply to your brand. Using a grid like the one above, disassemble your brand. Break it into the different equities you think it owns and place them wherever you believe they belong on the grid. Now ask some of your core customers to do the same. Then ask some of your prospects.

Next, look at the results. Which equities seem to be most differentiated and compelling from each of these three perspectives? If you're lucky, all three perspectives have yielded the same result. Those are the equities that can be the starting point for a highly differentiated brand position.

Equities that are compelling but not highly differentiating tend to be important "cost-of-entry" type equities. You can lose the battle if you can't deliver them, but their presence won't win that battle for you. The question is: can you infuse them with a sense of real difference?

On the other hand, equities that are differentiating yet not compelling can provide an interesting breeding ground for a differentiated and compelling position if worked and developed by a savvy marketer. The challenge here is to make what differentiates you actually matter to your audience.

Don't ask why, but I like using superheroes as examples when having this discussion. You might take the Batman brand apart in the way I've suggested above, and discover that while he has many interesting equities, the single thing that makes him different from other superhero brands (his competitive set) is this: Batman actually started with a purpose. He decided to become a superhero, then went out and acquired the skills and gear necessary to fulfill that purpose. Other superheroes acquired their powers, usually unwittingly, and only then went through some sort of angst-filled evolution as they decided how they would put those powers to use. This is how the Batman brand is truly different, and this is also why Batman is most compelling to kids.

When Apple launched the iPod Shuffle, a smaller, wearable version that held just 240 songs and allowed users to play the songs only in "shuffle mode" (i.e., randomly), you could understand how some saw this as a true product weakness. Surely not being able to play the song you wanted when you want it was anything but a compelling benefit. But it was most definitely *different*. So what did those smart marketers at Apple do? They decided to make the potential product weakness the defining characteristic of the product. Not only did that characteristic—shuffle—become the name of the product, it also became the sole feature driving the advertising. It was simple, it was different, and Apple found a way to make it extremely compelling. Genius.

To be both different and naturally compelling is a great position to be in. Different and not obviously compelling to you or your audience may just mean the situation needs a healthy dose of creativity, in terms of both strategy and execution. Conversely, if you aren't able to differentiate yourself, you're going to run into trouble sooner or later, no matter how compelling your product might be.

And while we're still on this topic, please take a pledge that you won't ask the following, question: "Who has done this before?" It's not that the answer is bad information; it's just that treating it as important generally stifles the creative process of creating differentiation. Instead, marketers should embrace the point of view that the only reason to know what other people are doing is so that you can do something new and different.

It ultimately comes down to creativity and nerve. You need creativity to make the intuitive leap to a truly differentiated position and you need nerve to see it through.

22

Brand Architecture— A Positioning Puzzle

Whether deliberately or accidentally, many marketers over the years have created what we in the business like to call brand architecture. These architectures are systems through which the customer can navigate the brand in question. Unfortunately, however, many seem more like mazes than maps.

I like to think of this architecture as an organizational chart representing one big positioning puzzle. You first have to figure out how to position each box on the chart so as to highlight and clarify its difference compared to the other boxes. In other words, each product or service must have an independent reason to be, or it has no real purpose in the architecture in the first place. Each box also has its own competitive set, and you must determine how to differentiate whatever product or service is in that box in a way that creates clear advantage against that set. Once you've done this, you must help your audience navigate the organizational chart as easily and intuitively as possible. (This last step generally moves you into naming and design work.)

You then must build your portfolio strategy, which is about setting priorities and choosing how to apply your resources against the architecture. Ask yourself the following questions:

- Where is your differentiated advantage greatest? Is it at the brand level, the portfolio level or the product level?

- Where are the largest current and potential pools of profit?

- Where are the best opportunities to ride cultural trends to success?

Based on the equation created by the answers to these and other key questions, set your investment priorities, then reread the chapter on building critical marketing mass.

A good brand architecture needs to be as simple as possible, but no simpler. When done right, it can be used to both attract and retain the customer, and to bring the brand strategy to life. Although smart brand architecture looks simple on the surface it also encourages the customer to participate in a deeper level of brand understanding.

BMW, for example, is a brand dedicated to performance. Anyone in the market for a performance luxury car is probably familiar with BMW's "ultimate driving machine" tagline. Many of these potential customers also know that BMW uses a system of numbers as its working brand architecture (indeed, numbers seem very consistent with performance). They also know that the larger the number, the larger and more expensive the car. Further, some even know that the first number refers to the series, or model (3 series, 5 series and so on), and that the last two numbers indicate the size of the engine (a BMW 530, for example, is a 5 series model with a 3.0 liter engine). This is as far as I'll go, but I'm sure that there are deeper nuances with which I'm not familiar.

It is a remarkably simple architecture that enables anyone to spot a BMW and quickly identify not only the model, but also its engine/

performance option. The system is beautifully consistent with brand position and brand lore. And once you understand the system, it is easily navigated and self-explanatory. Even within the cluttered car market, BMW's approach feels proprietary and differentiating, and is an example of an elegant and attractive brand architecture.

That said, BMW decided early on that its differentiated advantage was greatest at the brand level, which made its architecture relatively easy to manage. Customers decide they want a BMW—*then* pick their model. Those of us sitting on more complex, less well-managed architectures have a much more difficult task ahead of us.

When an architecture is proprietary, however, it can even be used to retain customers. A brand shorthand acts as the barb at the end of the hook, ensuring that whatever you catch doesn't fall off.

When it comes to the Levi's brand, fit and style information are the hooks for prospective customers. You look for the description (boot cut, relaxed fit, etc.) that you want, and then you buy the jeans. Once you find the right style and fit (the hook) you learn to use the number that stands as brand shorthand for this information (Levi's 505, for example). This is the barb. While anyone can give you a relaxed fit, only Levi's can give you 505s. (And if you are a purist, there is only one true pair of jeans—the non-prewashed, button-fly Levi's 501.)

As you think through your brand's architecture, channel the great architect Mies van der Rohe: be both modern and minimalist in your approach. Or, put another way, be more like *Real Simple* magazine than *Architectural Digest*. Be the iPad that needs no instruction booklet, not the complex smartphone that comes with an impenetrable user guide.

23

The Non-Sense
of Positioning

Marketing is positioning. Brands are a response to the stimulus of positioning.

Unfortunately, the art of positioning, particularly at the hands of brand identity and advertising agencies, has become too closely linked to marketing communication. As I've already suggested, a position is the most compressed form of the idea that represents your *differentiated competitive advantage*. It should sit at the very center of your marketing strategy and must represent the vision that drives that strategy.

A position must inspire and guide the entire customer experience, from employee interaction to product delivery to packaging to communication to customer complaint resolution. It must guide whom you hire. It must drive your product portfolio. It must even guide the CEO's speech to her kid's class on Parents' Day. If something will result in or influence a customer contact of some kind, that something must be informed by your position.

Put another way, the *position must be informed by everything and it must then inform everything.*

The historical link between brand and marketing extends to positioning. The result, unfortunately, is that our industry seems far too focused on the poetry of a position. We're a profession of frustrated writers and poets, and this writing and poetry can often get in the way of clarity. Poetry can be beautiful and seductive, but it can also be useless—just like a wonderful aroma wafting in from the kitchen when there's actually nothing to eat.

Keep in mind that positions are *internal assets.* They may influence the marketplace, but that marketplace will never directly experience the positioning idea itself. With this as context, doesn't it seem bizarre that many marketers insist on testing their position with consumers? The real test of a position should be measuring what it can inspire among those individuals (employees, designers, advertising creative folks, etc.) charged with translating that position into a vehicle (or vehicles) that consumers will see. Only later is that vehicle tested with the audience to determine if the position was successfully communicated.

This isn't to say you don't need to gain a clear customer perspective on a position—you do. But you don't want to have those customers caught up in the words. Instead, you want to explore the ideas and hypotheses that underlie the position. Every good position sits atop a few critical hypotheses: If x is true, the position makes sense; if y is true, it won't work. Construct those hypotheses—then fully explore and test them. Don't test the position itself. Test the execution created by the position—but again, don't test the position itself.

If you've been doing this for a while you've seen lots of positioning statements. Hopefully you love what you see for all of the right reasons. But far too often you find yourself nodding your head merely because you can't argue with a position—which is exactly why it could be dangerously wrong. I once sat in on a meeting where a leading brand identity firm presented the new brand position for a major consumer brand. After the big unveiling, the presenter turned to me and asked: "Is your thinking consistent with this?" After a pause, I could only answer "yes." After another pause, however, I had to add: "But I'm having a hard time thinking of anything reasonable that wouldn't be consistent with your recommended positioning statement."

Keeping in mind that you shouldn't literally test a position with consumers, another classic positioning error I've witnessed is iterative research that involves constantly rewriting the brand position until consumers can no longer find any fault with it. By that point you have something that is no longer (if it ever was) a celebration of what makes you different, but a listing of what makes you inoffensive. These positions are usually so bland that they have zero chance of driving marketing that will get any attention in the marketplace.

World peace is not a brand position. But if you test it, you'll have a hard time finding customers who are against it. In a similar vein, one leading technology firm was once sold a two-word brand position, and the first word was "intelligent" (trust me, the second word doesn't help). That kind of position is ownable and differentiating only if all the company's competitors positioned themselves with two-word statements starting with the word "dumb."

If I seem a bit intense on this topic, it's partly because I'm writing this a day after just such a meeting. At that meeting, a "brand positioning statement" was sold to a leading consumer brand. Not only could that statement be used by *any* brand in the category, it could be used by just about any brand in any category. Management bought into this brand position because the poetry was nice and because it was hard to argue with—and that's exactly why it's wrong. There are at least a dozen different strategies that could be employed—from smart and differentiating to remarkably stupid—and all would be consistent with this generic brand position.

The reality is that a position must guide and inspire. It must tell you what to do and—sometimes more important—it must tell you what not to do. And it must be prescriptive to the entire organization.

Take the History Channel. Its position should be somewhat obvious merely from its name. Yet several years ago the channel's two top rated shows were *Ice Road Truckers* and *Ax Men*—reality shows rather than history productions. Clearly someone at the History Channel has decided that the network cannot stay focused on history *and* create programs that draw high ratings.

That seems like false reasoning to me, but I'm an uninformed bystander. Perhaps it's just too challenging to develop great historical television. But if you're not going to stay true to who and what you are, it's time to change your name and admit defeat for your original premise. The problem is that most viewers who watch these shows actually think they're on the Discovery Channel. Why? Because those productions fit better with the Discovery position than they do with History. Surely, however, there are on-position programming concepts that can also rate higher than either of these two shows?

Positioning doesn't need to be poetic, although inspiring poetry can help. This is especially true if you're selling through an organization and asking people to live with a position over time. If you are a single (or master) brand, company positions must be embraced internally before any external manifestation is broadcast. And your internal organization simply won't believe a position unless it is brought to life across the company and in the product or service experience itself.

I say this because I've had my share of positioning failures. I've been in situations in which a client fell in love with the brand position I recommended, did the easy stuff well (such as use the position to drive marketing communications), but then balked when it came to using the position to drive the product experience itself.

Think of it as a test. If the position is not driven by the product experience, it's wrong. If you don't feel you can elevate the position into the product experience, then the position is wrong. The product must inform and drive the position. And, conversely, the position must inform and drive the product.

Here are some examples:

TV Guide wanted a new position. What it got was a presentation that demonstrated that "guide" was actually a great position—that the world has never needed a guide to television programming more than it does today. The magazine loved hearing this and readily embraced all of the positive implications of being *the* guide.

But then came the hard part: *TV Guide* now needed the products and services that actually could guide *today's* consumer through *today's* programming environment. And that meant some pretty dramatic changes in the company's offerings. These were changes that *TV Guide* was either unable or unwilling to make, so the guide position informed its promotional program and nothing more. The result? *TV Guide* was sold for just $1 a couple of years later.

On a more positive note, Unilever wanted to take the Dove brand and transform it into a beauty icon. A very ambitious objective . . . until you combined it with the belief that women were ready to relate to a brand positioned toward who they really are. The Dove brand, deftly positioned to feature real women with real curves, stood out because it broke what most believed to be the foundational positioning rules of the category.

At the opposite end of the spectrum, Victoria's Secret has built a large business by positioning itself as the lingerie brand for the supermodel that resides in every woman (and in the mind of every man). Both companies have built very successful businesses out of polar opposite but highly differentiated positions, executed brilliantly across absolutely everything they do.

While at an advertising agency several years ago, I found myself in an internal agency debate over Sony, which was one of our clients. Our global management and Sony's global management had agreed that a global brand campaign was in order—a campaign that would encompass all Sony products. In other words: when in doubt in the global advertising business, just go with the old global brand advertising campaign.

But before you can start creative development you need a brand position, and in this case we had a bit of a challenge.

My argument was that however you look at it, the Sony brand is defined by—and comes to life in—the design of its products. The second part of my argument was that people find it much easier to deal with a brand position when it's brought to life in a real product than when it's sold on a purely conceptual basis. The third part was that once you've raised the position to the elevation necessary to cover the full range of Sony's catalog, you are already off into the thin air of metaphor and analogy.

As an alternative, I suggested that Sony take the large amount of money being set aside for the proposed global brand campaign, break it into four, and each quarter put the requisite amount behind the single product that best embodied Sony Corp. in the most compelling way. Do this, I suggested, in a consistent campaign style, one that was imbued with the values of the Sony brand. Spend quarter to quarter and everyone wins. You'll still have a Sony brand campaign, I told them, but now you will be using it to celebrate the products that best showcase Sony brand values, the ones that best *embody* the Sony brand position. And since this kind of marketing is both reality-based and grounded in the product, the consumer will actually understand what you're talking about.

So what was the outcome? Unfortunately, momentum was already behind a global brand campaign, which was viewed as very different from a product-focused campaign driven by brand values. If you're in advertising, you may vaguely remember an ad with a painted egg rolling down the street. You won't remember much more. The campaign was quickly pulled and, to the best of my knowledge, never resurrected.

Years later, I can point to Apple as a compelling example of the approach I suggested. (Where were you people when I needed you?)

How do you know if you have the "right" position? Here's a list of questions that can help:

- Is your position a single idea?

- Is it based on differentiated advantage?

- Is it real? Is it true to the product or service experience?

- Can your position both guide and inspire your organization and your customer?

- Does it have a sense of mission? [Not all brands can or should.]

- If you listen, will it tell you what to do? What not to do?

- Can it drive everything that touches your customer?

- Does your position have a strong point of view? Would you be excited to market the idea itself? [I particularly like this one. Try putting together a marketing plan for the positioning idea without the product.]

- Does it have creative energy? Can you see an ad? What would the press release say?

- Can you see the position becoming part of standard organizational language? What does the line of T-shirts look like?

SECTION 3

MARKETING IS A NINE-LETTER WORD

(A Random Walk Through a Marketer's Mind—In Six Parts)

PART 1:
THOUGHTS YOU CAN
USE TOMORROW

24

Build Critical
Marketing Mass

If it's worth doing,
it's worth doing well.
If it can't be done well, it's
not worth doing at all.

— Proverb

Imagine placing fifty cents into millions of vending machines, all of which require a dollar before you can get anything out of them. In the end, you've spent a fortune and have absolutely nothing to show for it. You wouldn't do anything this foolish with your money—right?

But in business we're all guilty of doing just that. We spend countless hours writing marketing plans and brainstorming tactics, sometimes even coming up with something both original and brilliant. That original and brilliant idea then goes into the plan with all of the other original and brilliant initiatives and the budget is spread out across all of these smart things we think we need to do.

The problem is that none of these initiatives has any chance of reaching critical mass.

Why? Imagine a line that moves through time. Above this imaginary line you capture your audience's attention, below this line you don't. It really can be this absolute, since there is no such thing as *almost* getting noticed. I always preferred to run well below the line for most of the year, which allowed me to focus my resources and take at least one really strong leap above the line annually.

Limited opportunity for attention means that you need to take each of your tactics or marketing initiatives and prioritize them based on such criteria as strategic importance, marketplace impact and expected cost efficiency. Next, calculate the "cost of success" for each of these initiatives. This cost of success must be an honest and realistic assessment of what it will take for the initiative to actually work in the marketplace, for your audience to seriously consider it. Be sure to err on the high side, as it's easy to underestimate how much it takes to get attention from real people out there in the real world.

Now, running down your priorities one at a time, determine how many can you afford before your budget runs out. These should be the only projects that get the green light. *Do it to effect or don't do it at all needs to be your guiding philosophy.*

Once again, be absolutely ruthless with your priority setting. Be honest about what it will really take to beat a competitor and to grab your target audience's attention. You'll end up doing less as a result, but you'll do better. And a natural side benefit of doing less is that you'll execute more effectively on the initiatives that do make the grade.

All of this is just common sense. So why is it so hard to do?

Answer: politics and organizational structure. Different groups want their slice of the budget and it's hard to say no. A leading retailer with whom I worked closely many years ago had a marketing budget well in excess of $500 million. Lots of potential for critical mass there. But by the time each department and sub-department had been allocated its portion, critical mass was nowhere to be found. A few million dollars here, a few million there, and before you knew it the money was gone.

This is exactly the wrong approach, because for all that money spent, no single initiative ever rose above that invisible attention-getting line. Had the company focused the budget on a smaller number of high priority marketing programs, it could have had a huge marketplace impact throughout the year.

The task, then, is to create critical mass, somehow, somewhere, sometime.

None of us have unlimited resources, and to some marketers the notion of real, critical marketing mass might seem like a dream. But that's an error of perspective. They haven't yet accepted the fact that it's better to get noticed by one person than to get almost noticed by thousands. Instead, they are all too content to forever fall short. It's the CFO's fault—right?

So how do you actively create critical mass?

- Believe in what you've just read here and apply it ruthlessly
- Limit your core audience
- Limit your geography
- Limit the time frame
- Limit the media mix
- Limit the vehicles used within the selected medium, even if it means advertising in a single television program. (But own that show!)

In other words, always *own* a slice of a communications channel—and therefore of your prospect's attention—no matter how thin that slice might be. Then use success on that narrow front to gain a bigger budget and thicker slice.

At the same time, actively test a couple of the proposed initiatives that didn't make the cut. Test them in a limited geography, in a limited time frame or against a limited audience. However you do it, get a sense of their potential. If anything comes up positive, flag those initiatives for next year's critical mass priority list.

25

Stop Thinking
Outside the Box

I f niche marketing is the most misdirected object of contempt in my profession, then "thinking outside the box" is the most misdirected object of admiration.

In fact, the box is the strategy.

The truth is, any idiot can think outside the box. You can make noise there, but it's irrelevant. To be fair, the most unimaginative manager can easily stay in the middle of the box. It may be relevant, but it's awfully quiet in there. The real challenge is to punch the hell out of the edges of that box—from the inside, because that's the only way to change the size or shape of that box.

You spent a lot of time building that box, so why abandon it now? Spend too much time outside the box and everyone gets confused. Moreover, the position gradually loses relevance as too many creatively driven tactics assault the customer. In the end, while going outside the box is almost always presented as brilliant rebellion, it is, in fact, the easier road to take and a recipe for failure.

Of course, executing from the center of the box can be just as harmful. The center is obvious. The center is boring and expected. More important, playing around in the center of the box doesn't make any noise—no one notices—and it certainly doesn't change the size or shape of the box.

Moving from strategy to execution, it's always interesting to review creative work inside an ad agency. You sit there with the creative strategy in hand (the box) and, too often, see brilliant, creative ideas that are completely disconnected from that strategy. When these ideas make it on air we're left scratching our heads. You also see ideas that you could have written yourself (i.e., on strategy but nonetheless lame). When they make it on air you simply don't notice.

In my experience, creative ideas are easy to come by and strategic ideas are the all-too-common, safe fallback. Meanwhile, ideas that deliver the strategy in a highly creative, intriguing way are few and far between—and all the more valuable because of their rarity.

Again, your task is to create innovative and fresh ways to punch the edges of that box from the inside out. Hit those edges hard. This is the only way to make that box bigger, the only way to actually change its shape. After all, who says it needs to be a box in the first place?

Take Nike and ESPN, two powerful and highly differentiated brands in related markets. As defined by results, their architects were geniuses. Over time they have moved from strength to strength, and many layers of business and meaning have been added to the original brand and business definitions. In other words, although they never left their boxes, they have continued to push their own boundaries, dramatically changing the size and shape of those boxes.

In general, the boxes for these two companies are well understood. You might argue (and I certainly would) that their future successes will be determined by execution rather than big positioning considerations. Because they are already so successful, neither faces competitors that can beat them head-to-head, but both face smaller attacks from a multitude of more tightly focused niche competitors. In addition, these two boxes are particularly well maintained and remain flexible as the two companies continue to live with the questions that surround them as they move forward. Both are also served by an agency that "gets them," an agency that understands their boxes and how to make lots of noise at the edges. In fact, the agency for both companies is Wieden-Kennedy. Coincidence?

That leads me to another point: there are noisy boxes and quiet boxes. In other words, there are noisy strategies and quiet strategies.

Noisy strategies grow out of positioning that is inherently provocative. Positioning that contains a point of view, an attitude, and an edge. In contrast, quiet strategies don't make you think. They don't provoke. They don't inspire.

The volume of a strategy isn't about how loud the stimulus is, it's about how loud the marketplace response is. Sometimes the noisiest strategy is to be quiet. You gain attention precisely because everyone else is yelling so loudly. When you are confident that you have something really important to say, you might actually get more attention by whispering.

The creation of a noisy strategic box is a very real intellectual and creative challenge. Part of the trick is simply being honest enough to realize that your current strategy just isn't loud enough. Is the basic idea around which the strategy is built compelling? Does it have creative energy? It's only a great strategy if it makes for great tactics, so test the strategy by developing a set of tactical applications. Was it easy? Was it a fun exercise? Were lots of options created by the team? If the answers are yes, yes and yes, you might just be ready to make some noise. If it was a real struggle to create those tactical applications, consider going back to the drawing board.

26

Change

Change is good.
Change is essential.

The marketplace is a downward-moving escalator. If you stand still you go down. You only go up by running—hard.

Last year, on behalf of your brand, you executed a marketing plan. It worked well and the brand grew. But now that is old news. What will you do this year? Theoretically, if you do more of the same, you might hope at least to hold steady—but that hope assumes the marketplace itself hasn't changed and begun to work against you. The escalator is moving down.

So what's new in your plan? What news will grab the attention of a reluctant marketplace? What will make you worth watching? What will pull in the fence sitters? How are you better today than you were before?

In the good old days of packaged goods, P&G required that every brand manager develop a meaningful brand initiative each year, which was most often manifested by changes in the product itself. The rest of us consumer packaged goods marketers loved to emulate P&G, which is why grocery shoppers seemed to be constantly tripping over a sea of "new and improved" package flashes. The system was open to abuse, but the mindset was right. As they say in hockey: you are only as good as your last shift.

Change is good. If you've written a marketing plan, put it through the change filter. That is, ask yourself what is the one significant change you've created that will grab the attention of the target audience? That one difference that will cut through all the other "change clutter" in the marketplace?

But change can also be bad, particularly if it's change just for the sake of change. Change has a dangerous flip side, particularly within organizations with short-tenured brand managers (such as packaged goods companies). There's a need, sometimes perceived, sometimes very real, to do something different—*anything* different—rather than stick for one extra second with the status quo, even when it is successful.

If you're a marketer in a new job, do your brand and business a favor. Get to know it, intimately and from all angles, before you actually *do* anything. Then sort through all the possibilities and pick one thing that you can focus upon. Find the one thing that will really make a difference. The one thing that will make you and your brand famous. Focus on it and make it happen. Build critical marketing mass behind it. Execute it flawlessly, and only then move on to the Next Big Marketing Idea.

Beware those small, seemingly inconsequential changes to strategy. Beware the seemingly small trade-offs that are easy to make. Before you know it, the cumulative impact can add up to significant changes that throw the brand off track. Change is good, but only if you know its purpose and you can manage it.

Be particularly wary of those small losses of product or service performance that save money and seem imperceptible to the customer. Yes, that single change may not be risky, it may even seem like a win-win. But what if next year's brand manager (you're now a cost-cutting hero and have moved on to something bigger and better) makes his or her contribution in the form of a second cost-saving program, again with a nearly imperceptible loss in product performance. Then a third, and a fourth. While each change is almost invisible, before long customers stop buying the product or service; the cumulative loss of performance has resulted in something they no longer want to purchase.

In this scenario, you're long gone (and thus safe) if you're brand manager No. 1, but you're not a happy camper if you're brand manager No. 4.

I watched this process in action as a really young brand assistant working on a "luxury" cat food (you gotta love packaged goods marketing!). We had just replaced one ingredient with another, cheaper ingredient. Like good little brand managers, we'd done due diligence and knew that the taste trade-off was minimal. Yet as soon as we made the switch, we started getting complaints from cat owners. As is always the case, it's your most loyal customers who notice first, your best customers who write to you first. But how could they possibly have noticed something so small?

So we went back to our files. It turned out our brilliant little cost reduction program wasn't exactly the first. In fact, we were just the latest in a long line of "insignificant" trade-offs. We just happened to be the ones who inadvertently tripped over the "tipping point" and fell flat on our face. Believe it or not, many of these customers had tried the food themselves and were able to tell us exactly why their cats didn't like our food any more.

As customers, we've all experienced this phenomenon. That is, we can't quite put our finger on what's happened, but somehow the product or service just isn't what it used to be—and we quietly move on. No call. No letter. No purchase.

When all is said and done, change is just change. Good change builds. Bad change destroys. The trick is to recognize the difference before it's too late.

27

Find the Flow

Even politicians get this one right.

Brand momentum can be defined as a clear sense that the marketplace is moving toward you rather than away from you. It means that the important trends are working in your favor.

Momentum is probably most obvious in technology markets, where analysts and industry experts can energize a brand fairly quickly by designating it the "industry standard," thereby making it all but unstoppable. Over the years, Microsoft became perhaps the best momentum marketer around, single-handedly inspiring the term FUD (fear, uncertainty and doubt), which says a lot about the effect this company has had on competitors.

As we discussed earlier, search as a function and Google as a company have seemingly unstoppable momentum. In enterprise services the momentum is all with IBM. In software it's still Microsoft, but Oracle has gained ground in certain markets (and we're all betting on Google for a desktop disruption at some point). Siebel Systems had incredible momentum until the market cooled, when it gave up a lot of that momentum to Salesforce.com, a more narrowly positioned competitor. Similarly, Sun Microsystems rode the momentum wave as the Internet heated up, but failed to set itself up to withstand a cooler, more price-sensitive environment.

Perceived brand momentum is obviously important, but how do you get it?

The obvious first step is to position or attach yourself to a space or idea that is itself showing momentum. Then, if possible, take intellectual ownership of it. If that's not possible, find an important (from a momentum perspective) slice of the space and clearly stake a claim. Know the analyst community, the press and the industry experts, and help them to see you as a reliable expert on a market space or topic, no matter how small.

Momentum is an elusive quality. When you have it you must constantly nurture it, care for it, and feed it. Yes, take full advantage of it, but always with an appreciation of its delicate state.

The masters of momentum are the political campaigners. They monitor the electorate and opposition minute by minute, responding to every opportunity and dealing with every threat. They are intimately aware of and in constant touch with analysts, the press, bloggers and local party operatives, and are ready to respond to competitive efforts in real time. They actively worship the gods of momentum and the best of them have extremely sensitive momentum radar.

As scary as the prospect may be, you need to think like a political campaigner. Ask yourself: within my company and its marketing organization, how can I create the campaign mentality—the so-called war room—that politicians take for granted?

You've got to apply this approach carefully, since it can't be sustained indefinitely. When you see a wave of opportunity moving through the marketplace, attach yourself to it. Quickly pick your "campaign team" and start your run. Smart brands find the flow and are able to harness cultural trends. On occasion, really smart marketers are able to influence and even create cultural trends.

MTV made music a visual art. eBay created communities of shared interests and passion, and an entire ecosystem of services rose up to join it. Nike brought a hard-core sports ethic into the mainstream. Target made cheap chic. And Apple forever changed the way we think of music, then "phones."

If you compile a list in your head of brands that actually influence or drive cultural trends, you'll see it isn't a long one. You might also note that three of the most culturally influential brands over the last decade have been Apple, Pixar and Disney, each of which counted Steve Jobs as a key contributor. Coincidence?

Culturally influential companies didn't get there by accident; they were determined to build something new. While they certainly knew how to link their ideas to existing trends and behavior, they were also daring and brave enough to go it alone, all the while staying ahead of the curve (but not too far ahead). Everything about them was different and new and exciting in a way that made us want to follow. Their products and services were novel. Their cultures were novel. And they chose to market and communicate in ways that were unexpected and new.

Momentum will often be unexpected, arising in the most unlikely places. Trying to lead the marketplace is not for the faint of heart, but chasing it is actually a lot harder. Consider for a moment: if you were going to start a cultural trend, what would that trend be?

28

Think Before You Blink

Difference is created,
not manufactured.

This point was covered in a slightly different way earlier in the book but is worthy of further attention.

In his book, *Blink*, Malcolm Gladwell presents the thesis that we make intuitive, gut-level decisions about events and people in a few seconds (at most), long before we rationalize those decisions with evidence. Gladwell recommends going with our gut even more, and provides interesting research on why we should, as well as tips on to how to train that gut. The book is a great read, and while I whole-heartedly agree with the author's central thesis, I couldn't disagree more with how he stretches it to encourage us all to just go ahead and make whatever decision "feels" right.

At the other end of the spectrum is "Better Branding," from the *McKinsey Quarterly* (2003, Number 4), which argues that marketers rely too much on intuition. McKinsey is a great company filled with smart and highly analytical thinkers, but it really doesn't have a clue about building differentiated brands. It is made up of brand managers, not builders, and its style would result in a long-term (but extremely well managed) decline. Gladwell and McKinsey each make valid points; it's just that these points are incomplete and therefore misplaced when it comes to real-world marketing and brand building.

The real answer is that a real marketer and brand builder must do *both*. By that I mean that first you think, then you blink. In fact, you should think, blink, and then think again to make sure you can at least explain your blink to those around you.

Let me explain. Great brands are built through differentiation. Great tactics are differentiated and therefore cut through the clutter of marketing and everyday life. So if you want to be different—truly different—an intuitive leap must surely occur at some point in the process. No amount of analytical rigor will get you to a truly differentiated idea. You have to assume that if you can "think" your way there, many others have been there before you.

Instead, differentiated ideas, whether businesses, brands or marketing tactics, are *created*—not manufactured. Put another way, your gut is the best instrument for reaching a differentiated solution. If you assume you have an intelligent competitor (which you must), your head, and deep rational consideration, will generally just get you to the same neighborhood as your competitor's head.

That said, you're an idiot if you don't start from a solid analytical base. The real trick is to have the analytical rigor required to pull the situation apart from every possible angle. You need to know the inside-out situation. You need to know the outside-in situation. And you need to know what you would do if you were the competition. Analyze. Analyze. Analyze.

You next need to *structure* that analysis. You need to organize it in ways that others might not. To understand it in ways that others do not. I actually love to organize information in ways that might tell me something new. I love information in general. I just don't think that information, however well organized, is sufficient. Remember, these days, everyone else has the same information. As Andy Grove (of Intel fame) said when quoting his favorite professor in a *Fortune* magazine interview: "When everybody knows that something is so, it means that nobody knows nothin'."

That means that once you've analyzed the hell out of your business, it's time to take some intuitive leaps. After the science of marketing comes the art of marketing. And its job is to create insights that rise above purely analytical conclusions. Then, once you've developed a few intuitively driven hypotheses, you need to find a way to double-check and refine them with your customers before making any big marketplace bets.

If you follow all of this advice, what have you done?

- You've conducted a thorough investigation, leaving no stone unturned
- Knowing that others have also done this, you've used your analysis as grist for the creative mill
- You've then used this analysis as a springboard from which you have taken several alternative intuitive leaps
- You've asked the customer to help you select and refine the optimal direction

Knowledge➜ *Organization*➜ *Creativity and Intuition* ➜ *Proof*

Anyone can do the analysis. So assume everyone *will* do the analysis.

Any idiot can create intuitive leaps out of thin air with no factual foundation to constrain the thinking process. Don't be an idiot.

And you really are an idiot if you don't reality-check an intuitively derived strategy or tactic. After all, even your gut can be wrong (tragically wrong) and we're not playing with Monopoly money. In our work as strategy consultants, I tell our team that they should expect to think they "know" the answer pretty early in the process. In other words, a decent strategist should look at the situation and have a rough idea of what the solution will look like. But a really good strategist knows that there's a very good chance that he or she is wrong. That subsequent digging will reveal ideas that will prove any initial hypothesis naïve. Those of us who have done this strategy thing for a while have been wrong enough times to keep those early thoughts to ourselves.

Now you see why there are so few truly great marketers out there. You've got to be sufficiently analytical to organize and build a mountain of analysis, *and* you've got to be creative and courageous enough to leap off that mountain in the direction your intuition tells you to. Strong left brain, strong right brain and the courage and boldness required to pull it all off. Great marketing isn't for the faint of heart.

29

Build an Experience

A brand is a promise of
a customer experience.

This definition should be fairly obvious when you look at immersive or experiential brands such as retailers (and many services). But it is also at play in a more subtle way in even the simplest product categories.

In some cases you can actually take the experience apart and put it under the brand microscope. In more subtle cases, it may also require shifting your mindset from that of a consumer buying your product to that of a customer experiencing your brand.

How might this reorientation change your thinking? Try walking through a real shopping experience, from start to finish, with an assortment of your customers. Working with each customer, map out the resulting "experience trail." Where are the highs? The magic moments? How can you take advantage of them? Showcase them? Where are the lows? The dissatisfiers? No matter how small they are, how can you fix them?

I once walked through a bunch of department and chain stores with a group of women shopping for apparel. If you're not a woman who shops in these stores (in other words, if you're a man), you may not realize that the stores still separate their apparel into departments with anachronistic titles from the 1950s, such as "misses," "petites," "juniors" and "women's." Let's focus on "women's," which is code for "large." Now keep in mind that when these departments were created, the average size for American women was 8. In 2002, that average was 14. And this is where Women's Department sizes now start.

If you are going to market women's clothing, you need to see shoppers' body language and hear their conversations as they walk through the Women's Department. It's for "older, bigger women," they say, or for "my mom"—and the whole walk-through is a complete downer. The fun they had walking through the colorful Juniors Department (despite the fact that nothing there fit) is long gone. The worst thing about this scenario, particularly if you're the department store in question, is that just down the mall corridor are specialty stores such as Gap, where all women are treated exactly the same, regardless of their size.

Walking through a purchasing experience with real customers almost always yields a few surprises, some large, some small. Frequently, the moments of magic will surprise you, as will the dissatisfiers. Often it's not those seemingly more critical parts of the process that please or piss off your customer, but the trivial stuff that you might have overlooked and can easily fix.

I always hated shopping at CompUSA. Whenever I did (and the fact that I did just reflected the importance of location in the retail business), I sensed a retailer with no ambition. A retailer with no differentiation. A retailer whose managers never took the time to walk with real customers through the shopping experience that they'd created. But the height of my frustration came with a single event: being searched on my way out of the store. Had someone really done the math on this? Did the resulting reduction in loss through theft amount to more money than the loss of customers as a result of the insulting way they'd been treated?

Needless to say, it came as no surprise to me when CompUSA, one of the nation's largest retailers of consumer electronics, went into Chapter 11. I wonder if they searched the company's senior managers when they left the company headquarters for the last time?

Okay, so you've mapped out the shopping experience step by step and you know where the issues and opportunities lie. Some questions you should now ask yourself:

- How does each step in the experience hook into the next?
- How do you maximize the efficiency of the transition from one step to the next and thereby minimize the odds of competitive intervention?
- How can you deliver each step in a way that ensures that the trail consistently delivers the desired brand experience?

The next step is to map out your competitor's brand experience. What insights can you gain? Where are their customers (many of whom you likely share) most vulnerable? What are their competitive strengths? What are the weaknesses you can exploit?

Look upon your brand as an experience rather than a product or service. See it through the eyes of your customer. Pull that experience apart, get it right—both step by step and as a whole—and then put it back together again.

I know that this all makes sense if you're in the service business. All major purchases are experiences, from when a customer first considers a product to the end of that product's life. But how might this work for a box of cereal? Let's try it:

- Walk down the cereal aisle

- Pick a brand from the shelf

- Check out the ingredients and the nutrition guide

- Make a well-informed brand selection

- Finish shopping, with the box visible in your cart

- Take box home and place it on a shelf in the cupboard

- Hope that it's selected by your family out of a 4-5-brand kitchen inventory

- Place box on the kitchen table

- Pour cereal into a bowl and add milk

- Place bowl in front of you as you eat

- Close the box and hope it stays fresh

- Replace box when content gets low

I'm probably missing a few steps, but you get the drift. Yes, we're talking about a packaged goods product, but what if we think it through as a service instead? As an experience?

Yes, placing the box on the kitchen table carries a lot less emotional weight than walking into a car dealership. However, by treating this process as a distinct—and potentially decisive—experience, you can dissect it, run through it with real consumers in real life, and see how to improve it. Maybe there won't be any big "Eureka!" moments, but in the packaged goods business a few small insights can go a long way when applied across millions of boxes.

30

Make Yourself Famous

"I'm gonna live forever.
Baby, remember
my name."

—*Irene Cara, Fame*

It's okay; admit it. You'd like to be famous. You want to succeed. You want to make a difference. You want to win.

Well, act like it! I think that anyone with ambition wants to make a difference. That said, for some reason, most of us simply don't act that way. We're just not ruthless enough. We let politics, niceties, organizational structure and time itself get in the way of doing what it takes to win. We've all seen managers make the easier choice, one that leads to losing, instead of the tough decision that might lead to winning.

Over the course of a year, a typical senior marketer will face a host of little decisions and only a couple of make-or-break decisions. The trick is to make the little ones quickly and intuitively—knowing that you must only get the majority right—and then fix the minority that prove to be wrong. Bat above .500 on the small stuff and you'll be just fine.

By comparison, you simply cannot get the big stuff wrong. The trick here is to be completely ruthless. You can't take prisoners on these decisions and there are absolutely no free rides. Think about these decisions, but then make them boldly. Make them count for something. Make the big decisions in ways that might make you famous. The attitude is right, even if it's unlikely that you'll really become famous.

One illustration close to my heart is found in advertising. I'm all for ongoing "agency of record" relationships. As a corporate client, it's fine to have this relationship. Feel free to pay your agency well, but pay it based on performance. To my mind, these are "maintenance relationships."

But once every few years a business needs a new campaign, and good marketers know that the marketplace effect of such a campaign can completely transform a business—for better or for worse. Skilled marketers know this because they have seen it happen to others in the past.

They've seen McDonald's turn a few syllables into a more contemporary position, they've seen a real live "Jack" help save Jack in the Box, and they've seen a gecko transform the culture of an insurance company. If they're old enough, they've seen a brilliant positioning idea and a catchy jingle turn a light beer from Miller into a category phenomenon. They've seen Hal Riney build a car company into a cultural icon. They've watched Wieden-Kennedy help build a brand with a "swoosh" and a sports network with an insider's attitude. They've seen Ogilvy and the idea of "e-business" play a very tangible role in the turnaround of the huge IBM brand. And they've watched "Curiously Strong Mints" and "Where's the Beef?" become hits through packaging and advertising. More recently in the beer category, they've seen people sitting on a beach transform Corona, and "The Most Interesting Man in the World" push an unknown brand called Dos Equis into the spotlight. They've even seen a brand on life support resurrected by the new Old Spice Guy.

If you're involved in the advertising business you know all about these campaigns and more just like them. You know that these campaigns really can happen and you know how they can transform a business. Sadly, you also know that they are a distinct minority.

So when you arrive at an inflection point and need the campaign that will make you and your business famous, you need to be ruthless. For example, offer a couple million dollars to the top three creative agencies in the country. Better still, locate the top three creative teams in the country and make the offer to them directly. Winner take all. The winning team gets a million dollars and bragging rights to a very significant campaign. Then, once you've got the campaign produced and ready to run, thank the creators for their work, pay the winner, and tell your maintenance agency to get back to work.

On the other hand, if the winning campaign idea is merely very good, and not the earthshaking concept you need, *do not say yes*. Start over, and over—until you are truly ready to make history.

Keep in mind we're talking about an inflection point for an entire business. For years your business will be able to operate from the higher base that will result from this campaign. Your campaign. How can you not do everything possible to create this kind of marketplace leverage— including putting your maintenance agency on hold and rewarding one of its competitors for a great idea? Your job is to succeed, not to protect the feelings of your partners. If you feel bad about it, buy them dinner and send them flowers. They're smart. They'll get it, even if they don't like it.

PART 2:
THOUGHTS ON
THE CUSTOMER

31

The Consumer
is Dead

For what it's worth, the term "consumer" really irritates me. I still use it to make myself understood, but it bugs me. With time, I've concluded that the word bugs me for strategic reasons—not just because I don't like the word itself.

"Consumer" conjures up a mass of people ready to blindly "consume" my product. And that couldn't possibly be further from the truth—especially these days. By comparison, the word "customer" seems more singular and implies a relationship of some kind. Consumers consume—mindlessly. Customers *purchase*—if they are treated right. Consumers are the way of the past. Customers are the wave of the future or, perhaps, a return to a more distant past. I know these are not the formal definitions of either term, but I think this is generally how they color our thinking as marketers.

This makes a difference on a couple of fronts. Right now, retailers have customers and most of their suppliers have consumers. For structural reasons, but also because of this schizoid mindset, the retailer often has a much stronger relationship with that person than does the manufacturer. Over time, this almost always leads the retailer to become a more trusted "guarantor" of product quality than the manufacturer. Ultimately, this means that the retailer can (and if they can, they will) source products and build brands that the customer trusts more than those from the manufacturer—and they'll be cheaper for many of the same structural reasons.

Most retailers have also become more sophisticated about their customers at a much faster rate than most manufacturers have become more sophisticated about their consumers.

The word customer subtly forces the marketer away from thinking entirely in terms of averages and large, faceless groups. That's why I believe everyone needs to build a real, working customer relationship management (CRM) strategy. Forget the software for now; just embrace the theory. In the old world, terms like *1:1 marketing, segmentation* and *mass marketing* were too often viewed as distinct alternatives. The fact is, for many marketers, inside their customer database (if they have one) reside customers who deserve to be handled 1:1 and can be profitably marketed to this way, customers who can (and must) be approached on a segment basis, and customers who can only be profitable if they're treated en masse.

Depending upon your business, you may even be able to use that same database to profile the unprofitable customer. All consumers may seem like they're worth having, but there are definitely some customers that you'd be better advised to send to your competition.

To illustrate: I fly a lot, sadly, and in the past mostly on United Airlines, where I was a Global Services customer for several years. We Global Services fliers contribute an obscene percentage of United's total bottom line. Lately however, for a variety of reasons, I've switched the majority of my travel to American Airlines. There's been no indication that United even knows I'm gone. Wake up, United! All you needed to do was query your database and fire off a friendly email to me as soon as you saw my business dropping off. CRM is not rocket science. Don't you want to know what's going on? Why has one of your best customers gone to the competition? Don't you want to halt my departure? Here I am at the door. Here I am walking out.

Nothing. Not a single hint that United Airlines even knows I don't love it anymore.

I think we all need to agree to stop thinking about the people buying our products and services as consumers and promote them to the exalted status of customer . . . and then we can all go back to fighting over them.

If you're a manufacturer and this creates confusion with intermediates such as retailers, who you currently call customers, I have another suggestion. Call them *partners* and treat them accordingly.

32

Your Customer
is a Cynic

s a marketer, you are positioning something to someone. As
we speak, that someone is changing his attitude. Changing her
outlook. Some of that change is just a result of his or her last
conversation with a friend and some is more deeply felt and therefore
permanent. One permanent change is that consumers have increasingly
adopted the attitude and behavior of professional cynics.

Blame it on the Internet. Blame it on the press or the school system.
Blame it on Wall Street. Blame it on marketers who chronically over-
promise and under-deliver. You can blame it on the government, too.
Blame it on whomever and whatever you want, but the undeniable fact
is that the modern consumer has become a professional cynic. And this
is most definitely not a temporary state of affairs, a fleeting reaction to
our times. Access to information and a broad range of perspectives is
the real breeding ground for this cynicism—as it damn well should be.

People "Occupy Wall Street" because they are losing faith in our
institutions. The more they know about big business, the less they seem

to like. In the words of GE CEO Jeff Immelt: "Businesses today aren't admired. Size is not respected. There's a bigger gulf today between haves and have-nots than ever before. It's up to us to use our platform to be a good citizen. Because not only is it a nice thing to do, it's a business imperative."

Two points. The first is that in today's market, product quality is less in doubt. The range of available quality is tighter. Big is no longer better. Meanwhile, small can mean handcrafted and suggest pride. Second, social consciousness is becoming a growing element of any purchase decision. With information availability comes transparency—the ability to see beyond the product and customer service walls of an organization to the underlying values behind them. Share a company's values and you are more likely to buy its products. Don't share those values and you are less likely to buy. *Really* dislike those values and you may actively work to convince others not to buy the product.

My point is that you need to respect and work with the cynicism of your marketplace, not just because it is to your advantage, but also because that attitude is generally well placed. It is emerging from information transparency (an accelerating trend) and, sadly, from corporate misbehavior (one hopes a more temporary trend). Respect the knowledge of your audience, and respect the healthy skepticism with which it views marketing.

To corrupt a much-used quote from David Ogilvy: The customer is not a moron. The customer is you.

33

Saints and Sinners

Always talk first to the people who will make the most difference.

No matter what you are selling:

- Some people love you (let's think of them as saints)
- Some people will have nothing to do with you (the sinners)
- Some people are simply on the fence (the undecideds)

This is the way smart political campaigns look at voters. You should follow their example.

First, know the saints and stay connected to them. Invite them to get closer to you, buying more as they go. If possible, enlist their help in building your brand and business. And engage their advocacy in reaching out to the undecideds.

Second, know the sinners and stay away from them. Trying to change the set mind of a sinner is a great way to go broke.

Ultimately, if you are interested in top-line growth, you are going to have to convince the undecideds. The sooner the better, because it's very likely they're also undecided about your competitors' products and services. You need to isolate those undecideds and get to know them. You need to know what their concerns and obstacles are. You also need to know where their brakes (fears) are and what their accelerators (motivators) might be.

I like to use movie marketing as an example. Assume that you're planning to market a sequel to a movie that did pretty well. Let's say it's the second *Lara Croft* movie. (The first had had some success, largely due to the presence of Angelina Jolie.) As the sequel approaches, there is a group of people who are going to go to the movie, no matter what. They might love the *Tomb Raider* game. They might attend all movies of this genre. They might simply be in love with Angelina Jolie. These are your saints, and you need to enlist their help in creating buzz around the film.

There is also a group of sinners, people who wouldn't be caught dead buying a ticket to a *Tomb Raider* movie.

And then there's a big group of undecideds, who can and will make or break the movie and around whom marketing be must mobilized.

Who are these people? What do they have in common? Why are they on the fence? Most important, how can marketing be designed to get them to jump down from that fence onto our side of the property? Is it all about the sex appeal of Ms. Jolie? Does romance with the leading man do the trick? Is it a *Raiders of the Lost Ark*-type adventure approach? For different (identifiable and reachable) audience segments—romance lovers, gamers, fanboys—is it each of the above?

It really doesn't take a lot of time and effort to find out. As a media junkie and avid moviegoer, I get the impression that most movie marketing targets the saints. But the saints are going anyway. So spending money advertising to saints only potentially shifts forward their attendance. The real money is in the undecideds—and too often they are almost ignored in many movie-marketing efforts.

34

Customers Not Marketing Advisors

Don't ask for permission from your customers.

There is a critically important and logical order implied when it comes to strategy development, a priority that is often ignored by marketers, strategy consultants and (especially) communication agencies. It is a simple syllogism that goes like this:

- Know where your differentiated advantages lie
- Know what you need to do to win the game
- Then go to your customer and find out how to win

Rely on business strategy, competitive advantage and marketplace dynamics to tell you what to do, *not* on the customer. Instead, the customer should tell you *how* to do it. Some consultants like to talk about "consumer permission." There's nothing wrong with that, as long as you are very clear on what you need permission for.

The only time you should ask a customer to tell you what you should do is when, despite every effort, you can't figure it out for yourself (a situation that all marketers do face sooner or later). But, long before that happens, there are a number of things you must do.

First, look "inside." Based on the vision and core capabilities of your organization, your competitive advantage and what you see as prevailing marketplace trends, determine the strategic alternative or alternatives that are best for you from a long-term, bottom-line perspective. I'm making this sound easy, but finding the strategy that brings all of this together in one idea is a real art.

Then—and only then—talk to customers to solicit their help in determining which strategy is best, and how to refine and implement that strategy. Will they give you permission? Where does that permission start and where does it end? What sort of stimulus do you need to get the response that they've indicated they're capable of?

Be wary of this idea of "consumer permission." It's great that customers think you *can* do something, but you're the one who has to use your experience and knowledge to determine if you *should* do it.

Of course, once you've determined what will work to your competitive advantage, you're still looking for the easiest path to getting it done. Customer research is all about finding the easiest path, in that it allows you to find natural marketplace momentum and use it to your advantage.

Put another way, you're crazy if you enter a fight without an idea of how you can win. Once the bout starts you have to take the chances that present themselves, but always with a plan in mind and the knowledge that when the other person plays the game "your way," you've got a much better shot at winning.

A client once came to us for help with her strategy. After a relatively short time, even before talking to the target audience, we determined that only one course of action could possibly succeed. When I informed the client, she replied that her company had done previous research and that its customers had stated clearly that this strategy and message did not appeal to them at all.

We persisted, arguing that there were no other viable options—and that, in this case, the right question was "Does this change your mind?" not "Does this appeal to you?" We then crafted some sample stimuli to test, and found the true customer response was "This message isn't very interesting, but it completely changes my mind." We now had a winning strategy. We had the active ingredient. But we still had the difficult task of creating communications that held that active ingredient within an appealing and interesting carrier vehicle.

Actually, their advertising agency had that difficult task—but we all knew it was the only road available and the agency came through. We built a campaign around that active ingredient and the audience ate the tasty multi-vitamin that the agency created.

On the other hand, Norwegian Cruise Lines once embarked on a beautiful, award-winning advertising campaign designed to entice young people to take cruises. The company essentially ignored the competitive realities of its own business. Surveys found that young people loved the ads—and so the campaign went full steam ahead.

But "Do you like the ads?" was the wrong question. "Will you go on a cruise?" was the right question. An even more critical question should have been posed to the older people who really do go on cruises, and that was: "Will this ad campaign scare you away?" Unfortunately, the answer to this last, unasked, question was: yes. Older folks stayed away from Norwegian in droves while only a trickle of young people took the plunge. Bad for Norwegian. Good for its competitors, who had stuck to marketing to (and showing their appreciation of) those older cruise takers.

This is not to say that there won't be times when you come up dry. You've looked at the organization, the culture, the product, the competition, trends and everything else you can think of, and you still can't see a marketing strategy that creates differentiation and competitive advantage. If this is the case, you're in a pretty precarious position. You'd better be either one hell of a creative marketer or someone who likes low prices and the margins that come with them. That said, this is when turning to your customers for insight may be the only thing that can yield the advantage you're searching for.

When we worked with Dove, for example, it was known simply as a brand of soap. The company, however, wanted to become a beauty icon. But while there was a stable of products available to the brand to enable this transition, there was no real source of differentiated advantage. So we went fishing . . . and got lucky pretty quickly. Many of the women in Dove's target audience felt that the category's communication style focused solely on beautiful models who were young and thin. In other words: "Not me or anyone I know!" With everyone else zigging, Dove decided to zag, and the highly successful "Real Beauty For Real Women" campaign was born. Despite the absence of differentiated advantage in the business or product, bold marketers created a differentiated brand point of view—a point of view that was executed beautifully by Ogilvy & Mather.

Or think of "Got Milk?" from Goodby Silverstein. It all got started by a truly brilliant planner named Jon Steele, who came up with the simple idea of depriving people of milk for a week to see what happened.

These are the moments when you see the creative side of marketing. It's not ideal, however, because marketing-based differentiation, no matter how brilliant, can be matched almost overnight. It also doesn't have the staying power of differentiated advantage that lies in the product experience or, even deeper, in the business model. And while it can be fun and rewarding, it can also, like Chinese food, leave you hungry sooner than you'd like. But, boy, is it fun to watch.

PART 3:
THOUGHTS
ON RESEARCH

35

Are You Feeling It?

Research is reality television for marketers.

As I've said before, only idiots and crazed entrepreneurs make decisions without research. A few of those entrepreneurs are legendary, precisely because they defied business or marketing logic and did what research told them not to do. This is how truly differentiated businesses are built and how many truly differentiated brands have been devised. This is why those legendary entrepreneurs were so wildly successful. But this is also why they are so few in number.

Smart marketers play the odds. On the occasions when they bravely ignore the odds, they do so at least knowing what those odds are. Smart marketers do their homework. They're not bound by it or held hostage by it, but they do it. You're not an idiot when you defy logic; you're only an idiot when you don't know what that logic is.

So do the homework. Do the research. Know your subject better than your competitor does. But treat research only as a means to an end. Treat it as a medium within which you can grow ideas, but don't in any way treat it as prescriptive. It also follows that you should supplement traditional and quantitative research with richer, more insight-driven qualitative research. Better still, don't think of it so much as doing research but more as an ongoing exploration of the marketplace, as a customer "immersion" designed to fuel the kind of insight that can create true differentiation and competitive advantage.

As I've already said, you must give a high priority to getting as close as possible to the real world. Participate personally. Get hands-on as much as possible. Stay in touch with your customer.

In the U.S., marketers and their communication agencies tend to live in cities such as New York, Los Angeles, Chicago and San Francisco. Within these cities they live in affluent neighborhoods or suburbs. Most of them grew up in middle- to upper-class households and in neighborhoods much like the ones in which they now live. They tend not to shop at Wal-Mart, not to ride the No. 2 bus to work and not to consider Denny's a big night out. In other words, they tend to be out of touch with their average customer.

At the 2004 Academy Awards, held in March 2005, host Chris Rock did a remarkable thing. He took the television audience away from the beautiful people in the theater audience and to a nearby Cineplex, where he interviewed real moviegoers. None of these people had seen any of the best movie nominees, and most of them cited *Saw, Barbershop* and *White Chicks* as the best films of 2004. You can fight reality if you're on a mission to raise the entertainment bar, but you'd better embrace reality if you're a marketer.

What then can a marketer do? Well, an admission that you don't really "get" your customer is a good start. Then, simply spending time in supermarket aisles or in retail stores and watching a range of customers in the "wild" will go a long way. At Kellogg's, I used to give our marketing team coupons and the task of spending a day in stores watching and occasionally trying to talk a shopper out of a planned competitive purchase. Their instructions were to use the coupon only if necessary. There's nothing like making a sales pitch one-on-one, live and in person, to focus the mind before thinking about mass market positioning or messaging.

Also, hire a company to conduct ethnographic-style fieldwork for you, and insist on coming along. Spend time with people in their homes, at work, on shopping trips. Our strategists often like to talk to people in "friendship pairs," so they're more comfortable with the process and more likely to call BS on each other. (In case you hadn't noticed, there's at least as much BS in reality-based marketing research as there is in reality TV.)

And do not—*do not*—mistake focus groups for real life. Recruiting a bunch of people from a database (most of whom have done this type of work before) and setting them in a room with strangers, a moderator and a two-way mirror is about as far from reality as any of us will ever get without pharmaceuticals. People who agree to do this for money cannot be considered representative.

Sometimes you need to run a focus group because of the task at hand—and as a fairly straightforward and structured discussion it can actually work really well. If this is the way you go, get a great moderator, one who really gets what you're after and is willing to push the respondents to honest answers. But use the results as input, not data. I often find that ideas pop up in back-room discussions during focus groups that never would have occurred without this input—ideas that ultimately make a huge difference. In other words, it's often not what they say, it's what you can make of it.

But, still, never mistake it for reality. For that, you need to get back out into the real world.

The closer you get to reality—to real customers moving through real lives with real feelings, fears and desires—the closer you are to the kind of insights that can really make a difference.

36

Drowning in Information

In the words of Rutherford Rogers of Yale: *"We're drowning in information and starving for knowledge."*

Most marketers don't need more research or more data. They need more insight.

That may seem a small point, or even an obvious one, but I remain astonished by the high ratio of money spent on research that *doesn't* lead to action compared to money spent on research that *does* lead to action.

Information is useless in its own right, and far too many people and organizations are satisfied with spending millions of dollars on useless information. Yes, you need to know what's going on out there—but only if you are actually going to do something with the knowledge. Only if that information somehow yields competitive advantage.

The missing ingredient can sound trite. Insight is a much-overused term in the world of marketing. But it's insight that you're looking for. It's insight that's worth paying for—not information. So try this: review every "research" expenditure you have. Ask the same two questions of each program or project:

- Will it lead to an action?
- Will it lead to insights that will yield competitive advantage?

If the answer is no to both questions, don't do it. Save the money and—perhaps more important—save the organizational time and focus that can be much better spent on insight generation.

Many companies seem to be so busy processing information that they lose track of its purpose. What if all that processing time and the minds that like to do that type of processing were replaced with insight-generation time and minds that like to create insight? What if?

37

The Importance of Why

You know the who, the what, the where and the how, but it all starts with the why.

It seems as if I've been running into this kind of situation a lot lately. The marketer has a ton of research on the customer, possibly all the way down to a working CRM model. The marketer also knows, from research that might range from huge segmentation studies to lots of highly creative qualitative work, what the customer thinks—of the product, the brand, the market and the competition.

In other words, the who and the what are well understood—but not the *why*. To me, the why is all about context—the real-life context into which our products and services must somehow fit.

Why do your customers do what they do, think what they think, and say what they say?

If you really want to get to the bottom of the why, you've got to be willing to step into the real lives of your customers, the real lives that will go on whether your brand and business is there or not. You've got to understand how these lives are working, how deep-seated attitudes determine how customers approach your product or service. This essential context is the medium within which you must operate. The medium through which your marketing stimulus must travel if it is to create the desired response.

Yes, there are trained psychologists out there with the knowledge and tools to probe the inner workings of your customer's psyche. Some of them are probably worth their weight in gold. I just haven't had the pleasure of working with one of them yet. My personal bias is that while I may be missing out on some deep-seated revelation, there's nothing I can get from a therapist that I couldn't get from a beer with a few friends. So, with this bias as context, here's a simple suggestion: just talk to your customer. Conduct a set of comfortable, natural discussions with your customers, and don't ask them anything about your business. Just talk about *them*. Learn about their hopes, fears, ambitions, attitudes and points of view. Just let go and don't worry about all that marketing crap—save that for a different discussion.

Now that you've stepped back and learned about the why, you should be able to link this context to the "what" that you already know. You'll find yourself much more confident as you move forward, able to leverage how your audience really feels and connecting it to what you need to accomplish in the marketplace. And the consumer, who hopefully in the course of this book became the customer, now becomes a full-dimensional human being.

38

I Like to Watch

Watch what I do;
ignore what I say.

Watch your customer. Just stand around and quietly observe. Retail expert Paco Underhill (a man worth talking to) has made a very good living out of simply watching people shop, asking a few intelligent questions, mixing in a healthy dose of experience and intuition, and forming conclusions.

Beware of the Hawthorne effect (i.e., once people know they're being observed they change their behavior). Only after you've formed a sense of how people behave should you start asking questions. How their answers match (and don't match) their behavior is where insights often reside. Why do they say one thing and do another? What can you do to take advantage of this attitudinal gap?

For years, consumer research told Kellogg's that our customers religiously read the nutritional label when selecting cereal. Does that smell right to you? The real-world approach was to stand in a few aisles and watch the process. Not surprisingly, very few shoppers took the time to even scan the nutritional content. But, of course, they want to be seen as good consumers and parents, so they tell us that they did.

I'm guilty of falling in love with certain approaches to gaining brand and product insight and, as I write this, watching real people shop is my current favorite. Combined with the notion of "brand as experience," I think there's a lot to be gained by regularly watching your customers walk through the experience you've created. Watch and learn.

Television ratings are a joke, particularly when they involve teens. We still rely on self-reporting when, even by simply observing a few families really interacting with their TVs, we can see that these ratings are completely out of touch with reality. The question asked is: What program did you watch? The question that should be asked is: What did you do while you "watched" that program? As we all know, viewers typically flick the channel changer at commercial breaks, making that program's rating irrelevant to whoever placed ads during that break. They might also be chatting, making dinner, reading or playing handheld video games. And these behaviors aren't important? In addition, viewers are increasingly watching through a DVR-enabled device, time-shifting the program and fast-forwarding through the ads.

As they search for insight and opportunity, marketers are even daring to go where no one has gone before—into the bathroom. Using a range of in-person and videotaping techniques, marketers are (discreetly) observing paid volunteers do everything from cleaning their bathroom to taking a shower to going to the toilet. (At least the researchers say they are discreet—I have no idea how you discreetly observe a subject wiping his behind.)

Consider the highly successful extension of Mr. Clean by Procter & Gamble. P&G seems to have done a lot of this sort of observational work, but the most striking (and intelligent) feature of its research was that the R&D people observed everything first-hand. Researchers were reportedly amazed to learn that real people actually dreaded cleaning the bathroom. They discovered that some people cleaned their bathrooms while wearing raincoats and rubber boots, old clothes and even while naked—all because they considered it such a filthy task.

I'm sure those Procter & Gamble R&D researchers already had a sense that people don't like to clean bathrooms, and I'm sure they'd read reports that also drew that conclusion, but there was absolutely nothing like seeing the real thing. As a result of those real-life observations, P&G created the Mr. Clean MagicReach, which was designed specifically to reach those difficult places in a simple, non-messy way.

Watch and listen to real people going about their real lives before you interfere with that reality by asking a bunch of questions—no matter how insightful those questions might be. Read or listen to Paco Underhill for more detail and lots of inspiration on this subject.

As the old aphorism says, look before you leap.

39

Do You Know How High is Up?

This one is simple in concept, but difficult in practice. You owe it to your business to know how high is up.

What does that mean?

Once you know the potential of your business or idea, you can build it accordingly. But to know this potential you must first get all the variables right. The product must be right. The product range must be distributed fully and merchandised clearly. There must be sufficient marketing mass. And the marketing message must be attention-getting and clear.

Unfortunately, however, business realities, competitive pressures and the perversity of life in general all conspire against you ever getting all those variables right. Despite this, you owe it to yourself to know the answers. After all, if you are passionate about your product or service, how can you stand the thought of never knowing what might have been?

The best answer is the simplest one. If you're a retailer, go find some stores. If you're a manufacturer, find a couple of markets. Then do whatever it takes to get each and every marketing variable as right as you can . . . and watch what happens. Don't worry about affordability—yet.

This is not a test market. It's the creation of a *perfect market.*

If you get everything right and it still doesn't work, then you can move on without any regrets. But if it does work, you now know your upside. You've now seen the Promised Land and can decide if it is enough. With luck and a lot of hard work, you may see it again . . . this time on a much larger scale.

Most people are so busy worrying about representative test markets and realistic budgets (both valid concerns, but not right now) that they never learn their true upside. Now that you do, is it sufficiently profitable or did you need to spend so much that the math just doesn't work? Can you preserve this same effect at a lower level of absolute cost?

Not everything is worthy of a perfect market test but many products and services definitely are.

An ad agency I ran a long time ago worked on a limited front with Nike. As it happens, the product was a line of dress shoes for women (and later for men) that used Nike's then-revolutionary Air technology. There were, however, a lot of issues with the rollout: Product quality was a problem at first (though that was later fixed). The initial styles weren't great (although they, too, improved dramatically over time). The line represented a new retail channel for Nike, and distribution was extremely spotty. We advertised, but not with much weight or consistency. And one might question the wisdom of starting with women's shoes and not men's.

If this all sounds like a recipe for failure, it was, and Nike finally pulled the plug on the shoes within a few years. But I have always wondered about the line's untapped potential. What if Nike had started with men's shoes? What if the styles had looked as great at launch as they did just before the line was discontinued? What if distribution had been complete? And what if the advertising (which was working extremely well wherever and whenever it ran) had some real media traction behind it?

What if? Well, Nike now owns Cole Haan, so maybe I'll find out.

If you're a smart marketer and think you're sitting on something with a lot of upside potential, you probably are. You owe it to yourself and to your business to find out. Don't leave yourself wondering what might have been. Test the ceiling and see how high up it is.

PART 4:
THOUGHTS ON
COMMUNICATING
THAT POSITION

40

Keep It Real

A product is worth a thousand words.

People don't deal well with concepts. They prefer reality. Brand positioning is a good thing so long as it isn't entirely conceptual. Instead, a brand position must be real, and it must be brought to life through the product or service itself. If there are multiple products under a brand umbrella, find the catalyst—the one that best exemplifies the position and makes it real to the audience.

All this is especially true if you want to change the way people see you. Yeah, maybe you can convince them you've changed just by telling them so, but wouldn't you be more certain of their response if you could present some evidence?

When Oldsmobile told you it was "Not Your Father's Oldsmobile," the unspoken response was "Um . . . yeah, it actually is." Oldsmobile had a catchy line, maybe even a good communication strategy, but it was completely out of sync with a product that really hadn't changed with the times. Cadillac, on the other hand, didn't need to say a whole lot about its new and younger outlook. It simply showed you the Escalade and—perhaps just as important—who was driving it.

Consider these additional examples:

- Target doesn't claim to be hip. It just is. No amount of claiming to be chic can substitute for the real-life presence of top designers and brands in its stores.

- Sun Microsystems may have been "the dot in dot com," but it was the Java programming language that brought the company's Internet-centricity to life, getting Sun into thousands of offices where it was subsequently able to sell a lot of profitable servers.

- You can say you're in the entertainment business and that intuitive design is important to you. Or you can be Apple and simply introduce the iPod. And then follow it up with the iPhone.

- Motorola called itself Moto and tried to act very, very hip, but it didn't work until the company launched the Razr. (Unfortunately, although the phone looked great, it didn't work well, so success was fleeting.)

Just as a picture is worth a thousand words, a real product or service that brings strategy to life is worth millions of marketing communication dollars.

The recent increase in "environmental branding" is a testimony to the benefits of making it real. Niketown, Levi's, Disney and Apple stores are all great examples of a brand being brought to life in a controlled retail experience. These stores are brand museums and galleries, showpieces that allow you to experience the brand at its best. A more recent trend is the "pop-up store"—a temporary brand showcase developed for the same purpose.

Initially a brand's retail presence is often a fairly pure brand play, and the profit these stores generate matters less than the deepening of the brand relationship that results from their presence. But then an interesting thing can happen. They work. They prosper. Why? Is it because corners weren't cut? Is it because the focus is almost entirely on creating a great brand experience? I'm just saying…

So keep it real. Never forget that a real product and a real brand experience are generally worth more than all the words you write and all the marketing communications money you spend.

Real product
+
Real brand experiences

41

What's Your Back-Story?

Almost all my thoughts on culture apply most completely to organizations in which the company and brand are one. But what about the consumer packaged goods category, where organizations are often built around multiple brands? After all, this is the birthplace of brand marketing. Such organizations are driven by management teams, R&D and marketing, not necessarily by the mission of a single and committed business entrepreneur.

Even here, I think there's a cultural opportunity, but one better characterized as the creation of a back-story than as the deep sense of cultural connectivity found in many of the examples cited in this book.

Consider a typical Hollywood character actor. This type of actor understands that he or she must be "positioned" into the plot, so one of that actor's first questions will be: "What's my back-story?" To help an actor understand the role and properly position the character, however small the part might be, an entire life might be created—just so his or her smile or scowl is perfect in that three-second shot. The ultimate goal is that we viewers, after a brief glimpse of a face or hearing a few lines, unconsciously assume an entire life and personality.

When Lexus and Infiniti were created, only one company built a back-story. The Lexus back-story was forged out of an obsession with quality. The dealer and ownership experience was built upon the idea of an organization totally committed to quality and attention to detail, and the advertising drove the quality back-story home. Suddenly, established, venerable brands such as BMW and Mercedes discovered that many of the rational underpinnings (i.e., excuses for an emotional and ego-driven brand choice) they relied on to sell cars had been swept out from under them by Lexus.

Infiniti, on the other hand, failed to build a coherent and differentiated back-story. Instead, it created a Zen-like ad campaign, complete with rocks and trees. It was a storyline with no depth. A storyline few could understand. From the start, and despite a great product, Infiniti was destined to finish second in this race.

The great advertising guru Hal Riney was known to delay advertising on a new beer until six months after the launch. He used the time to create and "distribute" the beer's back-story. If you look at the recent growth of the craft beer category, you can see the triumph of the back-story. Sometimes the back-story is real and sometimes it is imagined, but beer drinkers just assume that a bunch of driven craftsmen—people who care deeply about the quality of the brew they make—sit behind each and every one of the brands. At the same time, these very same beer drinkers look at mainstream beer as brands without back-stories. They see mainstream beer as all "front-story"—all marketing and no craft. In fact, that's simply not true. You can make a very good argument that Budweiser has a much better back-story than any craft beer, and that those behind it actually make much higher quality beer.

In the world of packaged goods, Crest created a successful back-story incorporating medical research and dentist approval. Tylenol did something similar, effectively using hospital and doctor recommendations as its back-story. Snapple marketed its (true) back-story as a small, passionate company as seen through the eyes and personality of its receptionist. Häagen-Dazs created the illusion of European ice cream. And every now and again, Gatorade trots out its real back-story, reinforcing its authenticity as the very first sports drink, one that was created for the University of Florida football team (the Gators) in the 1960s.

When Trader Joe's famously introduced a new wine, affectionately known as "Two Buck Chuck," to its stores, two competing back-stories started to circulate. (Whether the stories emerged serendipitously or were planted, I'm not sure.) The first account held that the wine was the result of its originator getting an incredible deal on a surplus of high quality juice—so high quality, in fact, that the wine industry was determined to stop its distribution, given that the $2 price was undermining everyone else. Good story, and apparently only marginally true. The second story floating around was that "Chuck's" wife, in a fit of anger, took his very expensive juice, bottled it and sold it out from under him at a loss. Perhaps an even better story—though even less true. It doesn't matter; what does matter is that, thanks to its price and those two back-stories, Trader Joe's saw the wine fly off the shelves.

So what is your product's back-story? Use this question to give your product or service added depth, texture and personality. And while your back-story needn't be completely factual, it must ring true. Think of it as the equivalent of Hollywood films that are "based on real-life events."

Products without a sense of back-story seem unfulfilled and lacking in depth. As a result, their marketers have a much harder job than do their counterparts who either build or inherit a strong back-story. No-history products tend to be more reactive than proactive. Their marketers find themselves changing direction and advertising campaigns far too frequently simply because there is no anchor amid the storm.

This shouldn't happen. Every brand has some form of true-life back-story. The trick is to build from that truth. Shape it and focus it—and then tell it to anyone who'll listen.

42

Attention—The New Brand Currency

"The only factor
becoming scarce in a
world of abundance is
human attention."

—*Kevin Kelly*, Wired *magazine*

A former colleague of mine, Ken Sacharin, wrote an entire book on this topic, and its importance today certainly merits a longer exposition than my own limited attention here makes possible. To me, his most important observation is this: Yesterday's marketing model assumed attention and focused on persuasion. Today's marketing model cannot assume attention and thus must find a much more subtle and interactive form of persuasion.

We are attention-challenged. Our lives are busier than ever before. Our view of the marketplace is more cluttered than ever before. Over the past fifteen to twenty years, the number of brands on U.S. supermarket shelves has quadrupled and the number of advertising messages we're exposed to has more than doubled. We've gone from a few television channels to more than a thousand program options. Thanks to the Internet and telecommunications in general, information is now ubiquitous. It is in the air we breathe. It is as available in Kuala Lumpur as it is Kansas City.

Add to all this a media marketplace where video games have surpassed movies in revenue and teens are spending as much time online as they are watching TV, and you can see why attention is today's marketing currency. Indeed, we are in serious danger of mass attention deficit disorder.

Entertainment has gone personal. When surrounded by screens and endless content choice, you build your own world. You never have to watch or listen to someone else's choice, unless you value their company more than the content that you would otherwise consume. And when content goes personal, the odds of advertising messages being part of that content decline significantly.

Some marketers already get this, but many still don't. For example, a lot of marketers still test their television advertising by bringing a bunch of people into a room to watch a clutter reel containing their ad. This is a research technique that was built in the days when attention could be assumed and communication accuracy was the prevailing question. Does anyone actually think this in any way replicates today's reality?

This kind of research, widespread as it is, only answers one question: if you're in a strange room being paid to pay attention to a television, did you notice our ad more than the others and did it communicate appropriately? Yes, this approach will tell you if you got your message across to those who were paying close attention. It will tell you how your ad compares to other ads that were tested in an equally artificial environment. But no, it won't give you any sense of that ad's real ability to cut through an incredibly cluttered personal media environment in the equally cluttered life of a real person.

Consider television, still the primary advertising medium. First of all, what was once a handful of stations now numbers in the hundreds. Second, we can change channels at the press of a button on a remote. Some channels (ESPN comes to mind) actually group their programming in a way that makes it easy for viewers to avoid the ad breaks during their favorite network programs. Third, we have TiVo or, increasingly, a DVR-enabled set-top box of some kind. Fourth, we have Video on Demand, content delivered through that set-top box and, increasingly, over the Internet, which comes ad-free for those who are willing to pay for it. Finally, we have television content flowing onto the Web, where we can access it on a wide range of platforms at any time or place.

In the end, an ad in that 10-rated program really represents something closer to a 2- to 3- rated ad exposure. And what happens when this reality forces dramatic change in the network business model? Today I watch *The Office* for free. Tomorrow I'll either pay $1 to see it commercial-free in a marketplace filled with iTunes-type services like Hulu, or get it for free if I select several ads that I'm willing to watch. Entertaining or truly informative ads won't need to pay me as much to watch them. Boring or uninformative ads will need to pay me more. The end result is that I will still watch my program—but when and where I want and under the specific terms that I desire. And only with the ads that actually have some utility for me.

Attention is the currency of marketing, and this currency is both hard to get and hard to keep once you get it. Worse, others are fighting you for it. This means that today's marketers need to be a whole lot more creative than their predecessors. It's a challenge, but it'll be a lot more fun than the old game of simply broadcasting an ad to everyone at once by road blocking the Big Three networks.

43

The Dollar Value of Creativity

Find the creative multiplier.

Here's the thing about strategy. The people who matter, your customers, never see it.

Real people experience your product or service—they see, feel and touch your tactics—but they never, ever see your strategy. The corollary of this observation is that it can only be a great strategy if it makes for great tactics. This one's worth repeating:

It's only great strategy if it makes for great tactics.

When I worked in the advertising business, every now and then I'd hear people both inside and outside the agency say something along the lines of, "Yeah, I know the strategy's a bit flat, but the creative team will bring it to life." That is dangerously lazy and wrong thinking.

Great positioning strategies are creative in their own right. When you have a truly great strategy or an inspired brand position, you feel as if you have an idea that is marketable simply as a concept—something that would be fun (and easy) to communicate just as an idea. You know that it is an idea that will provoke, maybe even disrupt. An idea or point of view that will demand a response from the target audience—even when it's still a raw idea, before it becomes a beautifully finished piece of communication. When you have a great strategy, you can already see the advertising, events and promotions that might be developed from that strategy.

Hal Riney created a powerful positioning strategy for Saturn. Yes, his agency did a superb job of interpreting that strategy, but the creative power of the strategy itself was the breakthrough that won the day. Once we had "a simple car that would return us to simple times," the ads and even the dealership experience pretty much wrote themselves. When someone in a long-ago meeting suggested positioning 7-Up as "The Uncola," everyone there knew that the breakthrough had been made, and that powerful communication programs would be an inevitable outcome. (Too bad that in later years they weren't smart enough to maintain the position and just keep its execution fresh.) Sterling Brands helped the Dove brand team create the "Real Beauty" strategy that has guided their brand so effectively, but Ogilvy & Mather (and others) created the communication programs that made it count.

Good positioning strategies are conceptually provocative. Intriguing. You can write a provocative white paper based on the point of view that sits at the heart of a great position. And good positioning strategies are marketing weapons in their own right. Great positions are in themselves marketable ideas. Great positions easily generate great tactics. So if you can't immediately see the path from a positioning strategy to its tactics, you've probably still got work to do on the strategy itself.

Once you've got such a position, and it's filled with creative energy, you can then move on to the tactics that make all that strategic effort worthwhile. And when doing so, never underestimate the marketplace power of creativity.

Creativity has greater dollar value in the marketplace today than ever before, given that outlets are proliferating while the content for them is lagging behind. Amplifying this value is the shift in the marketing communication model toward the need to capture attention. Just imagine people who actually want to see your ad. Imagine people telling others about how much they love your ad. Imagine people passing your ad around the Internet. What is all that extra exposure and tacit recommendation worth? In a world where you pay a variable amount to have someone watch your ad based on how much they want to watch that ad, imagine the value and competitive advantage of a great ad.

Also, consider creativity as design in the broadest sense—visual and verbal design. We've all had great design experiences. It might be the way an iPhone works or just feels in our hand. It might be the way a magazine cover looks and draws us in. It might be the way a Coach or Lush store opens in front of us. It might be a joke, a phrase or a print ad. Every now and then, as observers and as marketing professionals, we have that little epiphany. We smile—sometimes grudgingly—and mutter: "How did they think of that?" Or: "How did they do that?" Or, as is often the case for me: "Why didn't I think of that?"

Other than a love for marketing strategy, the thing that kept me going in the advertising business was moments like these. Every now and then, a truly creative "creative person" presented something and my response was simply: "How the hell did you come up with that idea?"

Somehow, that person had intuitively boiled down a lot of complicated and fairly rational information to a simple, elegant idea that had a completely non-linear relationship with that information and the resulting strategy. The idea was completely unexpected but at the same time—in hindsight at least—inevitable. At those moments you can only sit back in awe at the power of a truly creative human mind.

Remember what I said earlier: Anyone can be creative. Anyone can think out of the box. Similarly, anyone can stay linear, can stay right in the center of that box. Only a few gifted people have the somewhat schizophrenic talent to both understand the box *and* find its outside edges in ways that surprise and delight their audience.

I recently listened to Dan Pink, an author and a fascinating speaker. Like many others, Dan takes the fundamental position that if a task can be "routinized," you should assume that it's going offshore. Essentially, routinized means that you have the ability to break something into concrete, sequential steps and turn it into a "process." The corollary to this line of thinking is that creativity, in its broadest sense, will become *the* competitive differentiator in the new, Internet-based global economy.

What that means is you need to find people who are not only truly creative but also smart enough to understand strategy. You'd better pay them well, because they are few and far between and they can make a huge difference in the marketplace.

And that difference is going to get much, much bigger very, very soon.

44

A Nod to David Ogilvy

D avid Ogilvy is why I got into marketing and why I got into advertising, and I think time will prove him to be the smartest advertising guy to ever walk the planet. He was revolutionary for his time and if you now take the time to read his thoughts, you'll realize that he's still revolutionary today.

I joined Ogilvy & Mather because of David. He didn't know me at the time I joined, but then a strange thing happened. My first job was to run the Sears business at Ogilvy Chicago. A singularly smart, courageous and eccentric man named Bruce Beach hired me, despite my complete lack of advertising or retail experience, to run the largest account in Ogilvy's world at that time. (Bruce was, and still is, one of a kind—a highly differentiated brand.)

After a few weeks on the job, I got a phone call from a woman who claimed to have David Ogilvy on the line. Yeah, right . . .

But no, it's the man himself and he'd like me to fly through to New York to brief him on Sears. As anyone who has read Ogilvy knows, this man loved retail, and was particularly proud of our then-growing relationship with Sears. To cut a long story short, this very nervous new account guy briefs the legend, accompanies him to Sears, and is later asked to accompany him, alone, on a twenty-four-hour-plus train ride from Phoenix to Chicago. We talked the whole way and one of us learned a lot—though I am proud of the fact that David passed away knowing that when on Amtrak and faced with two really bad wine options, you always go for the very cold white over the room-temperature red.

David Ogilvy stood for great strategy. David Ogilvy stood for selling.

David Ogilvy loved direct marketing. Loved information. Loved accountability. David literally talked about a future where segmented customer data would drive highly targeted and accountable marketing programs.

David Ogilvy, the icon, took a lot of bashing in the '90s because a bunch of superficial and creatively precious advertising types interpreted his stance as somehow "anti-creativity." He loved creativity—but prized only the more difficult, intelligent and effective kind. Strangely enough, he abhorred the stupid, ineffective articulation of creativity. As I've said elsewhere, any idiot can be creative and any idiot can be analytically correct but boring. The genius is in commercial creativity—creativity that works.

David Ogilvy stood for creativity that works.

45

Assume You'll Only Get One Shot

If we don't have the time to get it right up front, how is it that we find the time to fix it later?

A quote I've used elsewhere in this book is "Having lost sight of our objectives, we redoubled our efforts." Another way to put it is: "Unsure that we had everything right, we spent the money anyway because that's how we planned the budget."

If there is a single message that I hope you take from this book it's that, in the execution of marketing, *don't say anything, don't do anything, until you're convinced that you have everything right*. Don't execute a communications campaign (i.e., spend big money on buying ad space or time) unless you're sure of your strategy and have perfected your tactics and tools.

Is that advertisement dramatic enough to cut through the noise? If not, tell your agency the plan is on hold (as is some portion of their compensation) until it is. The same goes for all areas of marketing communication. Needless to say, this approach will also add significant incentive for your communication partners to get it right.

Here's the important part. The difficult part. Have the nerve to hold back until you feel the campaign/plan is perfect—until you have no reservations at all about it. There will be untold forces both inside and outside your organization pushing for you to give the green light to the program. Resist them until you are ready. Don't be afraid of being considered an obstacle to progress.

Which seems like the more intelligent choice? To launch an acceptable (translation: invisible in the real world) campaign in May or to wait and launch a great campaign (translation: one that will get noticed) in July? Try thinking of these as binary choices, between a 0 and a 1, because that's closer to the reality of market impact than any incrementalist model.

Now, having said all this, are there times when good execution on Monday is better than great execution on Friday? Absolutely. Great marketers are incredibly opportunistic. In my experience, marketers are generally much better at recognizing moments when timing really is everything than they are at having the discipline to stop a train pulling out of the station simply because it's scheduled to leave.

Real marketing communication always does better when it moves from blunt instrument to scalpel. Blunt instruments need too much force behind them to work, while scalpels just need a perfect cutting edge. Start sharpening, and don't use the scalpel until you're sure it has that edge.

46

Advertising—And the Need for Radical Re-engineering

It was the worst of times; it was the worst of times...

(with apologies to Charles Dickens)

You've encountered much of what I have to say about advertising in bits and pieces throughout this book, but now it's worth bringing it all together in one place.

Media first. Once upon a time, the "target" sat at home watching television. Wives could be counted on to watch daytime TV and husbands came home after a day of work to sit in their comfortable recliners and watch the broadcast networks. It was ABC, NBC or CBS, and if you wanted to change the channel you actually had to get up and turn the knob. The audience was captive and networks really meant something. Family members got their news from the same television, but only when the networks wanted them to. They also got their news from a newspaper, accepting the time lag that came with the medium. Radio and magazines had a role very similar to the one they enjoy currently, though they operated in much less cluttered media environments.

Now let's fast-forward to the present. Television is still advertising's biggest moneymaker, but not for long. Channels have no real meaning. The Internet is being used to download a seemingly infinite range of content to your home, purchased or rented from a wide and international range of content retailers. It's a world that works well for the content creators and the content consumers who sit at the two ends of the entertainment spectrum, as the rights and the needs of both are (I think and hope) respected by the ecosystem.

Other than those channels that are tightly defined brands in their own right, such as MTV, ESPN and the Discovery Channel, the networks are no longer truly consumer brands. They have become important business-to-business brands. They both inspire and filter the content, promoting content that is worth the expense of producing over content that isn't. They act as a funding mechanism, or perhaps even a quality guarantor (think HBO or Weinstein). They fund and possibly endorse the creators of content, but their historical role of content organizer is rapidly running out of running room.

Just as technology can organize content to create personal channels, it can also link that content with personally relevant advertising—or no advertising at all. In this way, the advertising that once funded the networks has become just more content, and technology now plays the organizational role formerly played by networks and advertising agencies.

What about advertising? Well, those of us with money now have the means to avoid much of it—particularly when it's video. A 2005 Yankelovich study showed that 54 percent of Americans actively resist being exposed to or paying attention to advertising. An even larger number (69 percent) said they were interested in products that permit blocking, skipping or opting out of marketing. And it's still the early days of advertising avoidance. Just look to YouTube, Hulu, TiVo, Netflix and the endless number of pirate/bootleg video download sites.

Soon all programs (as well as all movies) will be pay-per-view and it will be easy to enjoy that view without advertising. A content producer will create an hour of great content and we'll each pay $1 to watch it. Those of us with less money will elect to watch advertising with that program—let's say twenty ads, paying us 5 cents each, on average, to watch. In this case our account will be debited $1 and credited $1 and we'll end up with free content. Those who are more passive media consumers will take whatever ads the program comes with. Those who are more selective will choose which ads they watch. Guess what they'll do? Of course, they'll choose to be entertained or informed, and will pick what they believe to be the best ads to do so.

In this future world, the old advertising model will be officially dead. Advertising agencies and direct marketing agencies are now one—they are fully integrated. Sadly, this integration came about not because of any great foresight, but because the agencies had no choice. In fact, they fought hard against it. Their media arms have become particularly fascinating places to work, being both creative and analytical in approach. They no longer simply place millions of dollars of advertising in one go, but *invest* funds driven by algorithms that push money toward effective advertising placements and away from ineffective ones. They are now focused on a range of tightly targeted advertising vehicles, all served up when requested by the best prospects, at the best times, in the best places.

As a result, the new communication agencies (you can't call this advertising anymore) are filled with bright young "media" people who have a blend of creative, technology and CRM-style skills. They're as comfortable with ROI and algorithms as they are with getting inside the psyche of their customer.

Nonetheless, creativity is more important than ever. The most entertaining and informative ads are more likely to be chosen by their intended audience—and need to offer less money to be downloaded—than will their less interesting advertising competitors.

It's a whole new world. And a whole new set of players will be making money in a whole new set of ways. It's inevitable. But describing this change is the easy part. Those who get the timetable and the exact steps right will make the money. It's a safe bet that the big cable operators, content creators and strongest viewing platforms will do well, while the content organizers, at least as they are currently configured, will not.

But who will drive the growth of the Internet as a delivery vehicle? What shape will it take? Well, at least perceptually, Apple (until now at least) has led the way, letting us download music and television programming in a closed-loop, Apple-controlled way. Surely Google will continue to help us cut through the chaos of content to find exactly what we're looking for—the reason it bought YouTube and created Android. Facebook, with more users than any company in history, will be there. Microsoft will never give up its dominance of the OS, and will fight hard to make sure it crosses over to all platforms. In hardware, Intel will do what it takes to make its processors the CPU's of all major delivery platforms.

As always with technology, those in the middle are in for a heap of change and, probably, a heap of trouble. As always, they will have to radically redefine their roles if they are to prosper. The countdown has already begun. It may be quiet but if you listen carefully, you can hear the numbers ticking away.

Yes, everyone is already betting on the big four—Apple, Google, Facebook and Amazon—but history also suggests that we keep our eyes on a range of companies that none of us have heard of . . . yet.

Just remember: the future is like a very fast jet plane. Once you hear it, it's already gone past.

PART 5:
THOUGHTS ON THE
NEW WORLD ORDER

47

Marketing in a World of Ubiquitous Information

I f brands are emotional shorthand for a wealth of information, what happens when all the underlying "longhand" knowledge is freely and immediately available? What happens when information is ubiquitous?

The Internet brings petabytes of information to all of us at the touch of a key, and will do so at the time, place and device of our choosing. This knowledge may be objective or it may be purely subjective. It may be demonstrably true or deliberately false.

As marketers we must manage the noise, we must recognize and deal with the lies, we must actively promote the truth—but we also must abandon the one-sided model of marketing known as *persuasion*. Product performance claims, made within completely one-sided marketing programs, will be increasingly transparent to prospective customers. And once the truth is known, those customers will feel betrayed . . . and they will *never* return.

I recently bought a car. After doing all my due diligence online I marched into the dealer to tell him that I would pay x for my new car and expected y for my trade in—and that if he matched my request we had a quick sale. The salesman sighed, we went to his desk and, together, we went online and quickly validated my research. We actually looked at the screen together as he accessed kbb.com. It was a purely information-driven transaction and therefore much more efficient. No selling involved, but the salesman still got the commission.

Because of the cost and importance of a car, we're willing to take the time (actually, no more than ten minutes) to do the research online. Clearly, I'm not about to do ten minutes of research prior to buying a bottle of ketchup or a can of soda, but…

On impulse, I walk into a retailer to buy a new pair of jeans. I find the pair I want, but they're $75—more than I really want to pay. I whip out my cell phone and, after a couple of button presses, find ten retailers in the same area, each with the brand of jeans I want, in ascending order of price. Faced with the evidence of a $10 difference just a block away, the retailer can agree either to lower its price or lose me as a customer.

I hit a supermarket on the way home. I've been asked by my wife to pick up ketchup but no brand is mentioned. Three brands are on the shelf, all at the same price. My wife is choosy. Not wanting to mess up (or call her and show my ignorance), I again whip out my cell phone and go to a site that compares different branded foods, objectively and through user ratings. One of the brands has a more environmentally friendly score, more real tomatoes and a higher user rating. Decision made.

Ultimately, shopping is just an equation that balances degree of importance against ease of information access. Soon *no one* will buy a durable good without first doing a little online homework. Many of us will go online to do quick research on higher-priced categories, as with the jeans in the example above. Not too many of us will check out ketchup—but some of us will, and they'll tell their "friends," and digitally accelerated word of mouth will take care of the rest. Thus does transparency become ubiquitous and universal. Transparency becomes assumed, and not making this assumption invites difficulty.

Your product doesn't perform? Your service sucks? Before you know it a quiet buzz will be felt on the Internet. This buzz of information will then give way to a couple of more influential blogs. Within a day—hell, within *hours*—a lot of hard work and good thinking will be completely undone by the very people you were counting on to build your business.

This is not a new phenomenon. Word of mouth has always been the most powerful marketing mechanism, but now it's accelerated and universal. We have more "friends" than we ever dreamed of having, and we are instantly connected to information, opinion and expertise, wherever and whenever we want.

Several years ago, a few young, smart people were traveling on business and were treated poorly by the desk manager at a suites-type hotel. So poorly, in fact, that they spent a bit of time doing what they do best—in the process creating a simple and hilarious PowerPoint deck that illuminated their side of things. They sent it to the CEO of the hotel chain, copying the desk manager and the manager of the hotel in question. Not expecting much back from the hotel, they also copied their friends—who gleefully forwarded it to their friends, who sent it to all of their friends, who sent it to…the world.

This was viral information at its best—or worst, depending on your perspective.

On a more positive note, if your product delights the customer or your service over-delivers, you'll quickly find the tide of information working on your behalf.

Your employees will create blogs, and you must assume that those blogs will tell the unvarnished truth. Your consumers will knock on your door and you will have to let them in—and they'd better like what they see. We've always understood outbound marketing; it's highly competitive but pretty straightforward. Unfortunately, the principles and best practices of inbound marketing aren't nearly so clear—yet.

Marketing is good. Persuasion is good. Brands count. But also know that the facts will matter. Those facts, as seen from several different vantage points, will be applied ruthlessly and at great speed.

48

It Takes a Village to Raise a Brand

G reat brands are built as much (if not more) by their audiences as by their managers. The manager can only create the stimulus; the audience filters that stimulus and provides a response. As I've said, only the marketplace can make your product or service into a brand. And if you don't get participation and try to force it, you'll only end up using a lot of real four-letter words.

Brands need the active and ongoing cooperation of their audience, particularly in today's technology-enabled marketplace. This means that the brand marketer has to give up some control to his or her "community." In some categories, however, the marketer can be highly rewarded if a sense of shared ownership with that community is created.

The Jordan brand is the best basketball shoe available, but that's not why it's such a big business. The Jordan brand is big because its community loves it. The community sustains the brand. Go online and tune into that community—you'll be amazed by its attachment to and involvement with the Jordan brand.

Smart marketers (and Nike is nothing if not a smart marketer) know they have to work with their community to build the brand. But they also know—though they don't always like it—that they must give up some control of their destiny to that community. And needless to say, they know that they must never, ever, betray the trust of that community.

Your community isn't naïve or stupid. It knows you are in business to make money. It just needs to believe you also have its best interests at heart. It wants to know that you truly share its passion.

eBay is a fascinating case of a closely integrated community building a business and brand. Part of the genius of the eBay model was that it had a massive network of unsalaried brand advocates and business strategists, all deliberately or inadvertently dreaming up ways to develop new revenue sources and to deepen brand loyalty.

As eBay has grown, the eBay community has given way to a loosely aligned eBay "nation" filled with thousands of communities that have built up around specific passion points. From almost day one, each of these communities has had an equally passionate champion within eBay itself.

Assume that your community is more akin to a village than a city—one in which everyone knows everyone else. If you are going to be welcome in that village, you will need to learn the language of that village. You need to understand how the village operates. You need to get to know your brand's village elders—and meet with them. They are wise and they are passionate, and they love to talk about your brand and the village it lives within.

Finally, keep in mind that you should never try to directly influence those elders, although you certainly should embrace them and learn from them. In turn, your own wisdom and passion will be passed on to the village and you will be repaid many times over.

49

The Truth Will
Win Out—Sooner
Not Later

Immediate access to "the world's information" means a bit of re-training for those of us who grew up in the one-way persuasion school of marketing. The task before us is to adjust to the much more challenging "interactive-objective" school of marketing.

In the good old days, it was our one-way persuasive message against that of our competitor. Who was louder? Who was more interesting? Who was more persuasive?

Today, within an increasingly wide range of categories, it really doesn't matter what we claim because our audience can easily find out how our product or service actually performs. Claims are now more like signals, alerting the customer to what the marketer thinks is the most important issue among many. You highlight your claim, they check it out. They may check it out with friends, peer groups, objective third parties or simply through a direct product comparison. . . but trust me, if it's at all important to them, they'll check it out. And if you've misled them in any way, they'll know. If you've misled them, they'll leave—and they won't be back.

This last "they're not coming back" observation is important. Too often, marketers act as if there are only two possible outcomes to an activity on their part—it works or it doesn't—a one or a zero. If only life were that simple and binary. But the reality is that if you set up an expectation you can't meet or, worse, you actively mislead, you may never see those customers again. No matter what you say or do, they will be lost to you forever—and even the quietest of them will take a few friends with them.

That turns the zero into something closer to a minus one—then a minus ten.

So accept that new reality and make the most of it. Learn how to use truth as a marketing tool.

A few years ago a BMW die-hard compared the official BMW website to his favorite BMW enthusiast site. At the time, the BMW site was recognized as being at the leading edge of the art. But this person's perspective was different. He liked the corporate site, but found it too one-sided, too perfect and too sleek. The site was great and all the cars were presented as "ultimate driving machines." By comparison, on the enthusiast site, the point of view was more "real," more down to earth. The contributors loved the brand, but they loved it in its entirety—warts and all. They didn't shy away from the imperfections. If anything they celebrated them. The net result was a much more honest, emotionally engaging and deeper conversation about the BMW brand.

There's nothing wrong with perfection, but don't allow it to blind you to passion.

Jaguar used to be a mechanical and electrical nightmare, but it was still a brand that inspired passion. Ford's acquisition helped turn Jaguar into a smooth-running, well-engineered machine, but somewhere along the line the passion was lost. Based on the added volume of the entry-level Ford Taurus-like X Series, sales (but not profits) rose compared to Jaguar's darkest days, but the once-obsessive, almost xenophobic customer base of the British years was now long gone. There are lots of high quality luxury cars, but there *was* only one Jaguar.

Of course, high quality *and* passion is the ideal and, in theory, high quality is more difficult to attain than high passion. But theory is clearly not practice, and the passion may never come back to this once-proud brand.

50

Catch a Virus

Word of mouth has always been the best marketing mechanism. It always will be the best marketing mechanism.

J ust take a look at this chart from the U.K.'s Henley Centre, which puts numbers to something we inherently know.

Which sources of information are trusted?	
Husband/wife/partner	90%
Friends	82%
Work colleagues	69%
TV news	50%
Retailers	27%
Manufacturers	27%
Governments	14%
Advertising	14%

This is not exactly news. People trust people they know more than people they don't know. This is particularly true when the people they don't know have a vested interest. And it is especially true if those people are involved in that nasty business of advertising.

Thanks to technology, word of mouth is on steroids. Technology makes word of mouth—these days called *viral marketing*—a very potent ally of great products and smart marketers … and a very potent threat to bad products and ham-fisted marketers.

It takes a deft, patient hand to effectively manage a viral marketing effort. Think of it as a set of concentric circles. As you move outward you find bigger circles made up of less influential people. Meanwhile, packed very densely together at the bullseye are a handful of *super-influentials.*

Depending upon the task at hand, these super-influentials might be anyone from a movie star to a rapper to a passionate person with a well-read blog. By definition, a marketing virus must start slowly and while you can start the process, your management of that expansion process must range from loose to nonexistent. Be very, very patient; sometimes it's better to fail than to succeed and have it all blow up in your face.

Viral can be good, but viral can also be bad. Monitor the marketplace vibe. Pay for a good search tool to scan the Web to alert you whenever people start to work against you and your strategy. Get on top of it early and often. Fight back, but softly and from a position of truth. If you try to bullshit someone in this arena, it most definitely will come back to haunt you.

Viral marketing certainly fits some tasks better than others, but has a place within a surprisingly wide range of categories. It's cheap, so just go through the process of applying it to your business—then decide whether to actively use it as part of your marketing plan. But don't dismiss it before you've fully explored its potential. And whatever you decide, don't ignore the potential harm that can be accomplished virally if you're not sufficiently on guard.

Perhaps the masterpiece of all viral marketing efforts was the word-of-mouth Internet campaign organized by those tricky people behind *The Blair Witch Project.* The movie was average, at best, but because such mystique had been built up around it before its premiere, by the time everyone realized the mediocrity of the movie, it had already made more than $100 million.

Tellingly, there have been a number of accidental viral marketing events. For example, the television drama *24* had its hero use a specific cell phone number. Hardcore fans paused the show when they saw the number, then actually tried it. It turned out that, as a joke, the writers had used one of the crew members' cell number. As the phone rang continuously, crew and cast took turns answering. It was all very spontaneous, and it felt that way—and because of that, the number spread like wildfire on the Web. Expect to see a whole lot more of this kind of thing—now planned as part of a larger marketing effort—in the years to come.

Don't forget: Soft hands. Deft touch. Patience. Truth. And luck.

51

Market to the Brand Broadcaster

Are you tuned in?

Marketers talk a lot about people we call influencers. Depending on the industry in which you work, you may hear them referred to as trend leaders, gadget geeks, early adopters/adapters or fashionistas. The implication is that there is a group of people in each market whose knowledge and passion for the category makes them worth more than their weight in gold thanks to the influence they can have on people who are not as "category involved" as they are.

Talk to urban African-American kids about their jeans and you'll get a real eye opener. You'll be blown away by how knowledgeable these kids are. They are "denimologists" of the highest order; they own several pairs and are able to tell you exactly what each of the brands is all about. You'll also be taken aback by how unabashed they are about their influences, as you can see from the following comment: "I tape the Billboard Awards show, look for my favorite artist, pause the tape and check out which label they're wearing. Then I tell all my friends and we go out and buy it."

Rap star (super-influencer) motivates urban fan (broadcaster), who motivates friends (influencers), who in turn influence a bunch of less category-involved suburban white kids.

Influencers might lead because of passion and knowledge, or they might lead because of status. Hip-hop artists are huge influencers across all kinds of categories, from cars to liquor to clothes. Movie stars can make or break brands. These people, and others, influence us because they have access to media. They can easily broadcast their tastes.

But media is quickly being democratized by vehicles that go by such mash-up names as blog, vlog and podcast. Personal playlists can be marketable commodities. In theory at least, everyone can be a broadcaster of some kind. Anyone and everyone can lead—so long as others choose to watch, listen or read.

These days, broadcasters are simply people who pass on their thoughts, opinions and passions to others. The number of those others represents the order of magnification these broadcasters can bring to their ideas. They can help you disproportionately, but they can also hurt you to the same order of magnitude.

In theory, each of us has a *purchase potential index*—a number between 1 and 10 that represents the likelihood of us buying the product or service in question. Each of us also has a theoretical *broadcast index*—a number that represents the likelihood of us telling others what we think of the product or service in question. Broadcasters hold court at social events or with a group of friends. Broadcasters don't just use the products and services they love, they "demonstrate" them to whoever is willing to listen. This was always true, of course, but technology-savvy broadcasters found ways to extend their reach. These days, however, you really don't need much in the way of technology savvy to become an electronic broadcaster.

In many categories, these citizen broadcasters will soon become the most important population of influencers. Know what they look like, have someone dedicated to reading their blogs, and realize that broadcasters can work against you as easily as they can work for you.

At some point, perhaps we'll be assessing media plans on their "cost per broadcaster" as well as their "cost per point of purchase," having long ago done away with such archaic terms as "cost per thousand."

PART 6:
JUST THOUGHTS

52

Marketing is Judo Not Karate

Unless you have unlimited resources, lots of time and a penchant for failure, do not fight your marketplace. Figuratively speaking, marketers should always try to avoid using "karate"—that is, fighting force with force. Instead, they should use "judo"—finding the momentum that already exists in the marketplace and using it to their advantage.

How do you practice judo? First, establish what you need to do, then find a way to link that goal to a greater marketplace truth. Put another way: Fit what you want the customer to think and feel into what the customer already thinks and feels. Find the momentum already in the marketplace, then find a way to leverage it to your advantage.

Get the head nod from your customer. The wry smile. Even grudging acceptance. While sometimes it's unavoidable, in general anything is better than trying to "convince" a customer to change his or her mind.

A few examples to illustrate my point:

- For years, Kellogg's spent its marketing dollars on core brands such as Corn Flakes. But when the high-fiber craze erupted worldwide, money was shifted into high-fiber products such as All Bran and Raisin Bran, which had traditionally been "quiet" brands. Business went through the roof.

- Starwood Hotels decided that travelers really weren't asking for much—a great bed, great pillows and high-speed Internet access. It "branded" these key features and very effectively sold them back to those same travelers.

- Surely, a few years back, someone other than Toyota saw high gas prices in our future. Nonetheless, as far as most consumers are concerned, Prius effectively "owns" the hybrid idea. That's because the company sensed the "green" shift in customer attitudes and came to market with an incredibly well-designed car just as that wave hit. Meanwhile, many of their competitors were still trying to push water uphill by shoving marketing dollars and discounts behind gas-guzzling SUV's. I'll never forget an interview with a senior executive of a U.S. car company who noted that "we were really caught by surprise by the downturn in truck and SUV sales." Seriously?

- Dockers may be well off the boil today, but once upon a time a very smart marketer essentially placed a brand bet on the "dress casualization" of the American workplace. As a result, Dockers rode the Casual Friday wave to success.

This judo philosophy of marketing applies to both attitudes and behavior. Always look for ways to track your desired attitude or behavior against what people already think and do. Radical new concepts may stimulate the imagination of the marketer, but if they don't track for the consumer, they won't track for the business.

For example, TiVo wasted a huge amount of money and, more important, time trying to convince us that we wanted some form of media revolution. All we wanted was a simple-to-use VCR.

As well as understanding the psychology and behavior of your audience, you can also apply this judo on a more macro level. In particular, find a marketplace trend that might be used to make a compelling case for your product or service. Then climb the crest of that trend wave and work it to your advantage. Position yourself neither too far forward nor not too far back. If you can do that, and you've got the right wave, you are in for the ride of your life.

Sun rode the Internet tsunami like a champion surfer, using the currency of Java to get in the door and then, once in the building, selling a ton of high-end servers. Sure, the wave eventually crashed, but you can still admire how well the company rode it when the surf was up.

On the other hand, consider Plantronics. Why is that company not riding the communication and entertainment explosion with its headsets? Sure, Plantronics is on the wave—but it's not riding it.

Of course, if judo marketing were easy, everyone would be doing it. In fact, this technique requires that you really know your prospects, what they think and feel, and how they are reacting to the waves flowing through the marketplace. It requires that you know what those waves are and, most important, how to translate them into ideas that can drive your business forward. This takes a real commitment to market research—but research in the field, because it's hard to spot shifts in the zeitgeist by hanging out at corporate headquarters.

Know the marketplace and know your audience. Know where the momentum lies. Know where the leverage is and constantly look for ways to use it to your advantage . . . and then make your move before someone else does. It's as true in the marketplace as it is on the practice mat.

53

If It's Not Important Enough to Win, You'll Lose

Competition may not be war, but it's not a game either—even though it's a lot of fun.

Competition is tough and often brutal—it's not for the faint of heart or the politically correct.

Competition creates winners and losers—and the dollar difference between the two can be astronomical.

Be the competition, don't just talk about them.

In my early days as a packaged goods marketer, I remember the annual high stakes game of writing the marketing plan. We always segmented our plan into the different elements of the marketing mix. If we were smart, we also prepared a section on the competition. The problem was that we tended to report on the competition as if it were an object fixed in time and space. An object with a brain, perhaps, but just not as smart or creative as we were. An object largely built of facts and figures rather than any real understanding and empathy.

One year I wised up. I created three teams to represent our three major competitors. Each team consisted of managers representing finance, sales, R&D, marketing and ad agencies. Each had two weeks to go to school on its designated competitor and learn all it could until it *became* that competitor. The final task was to outline a ten-point plan to attack our business.

We set it up as a competition in two parts. The team that compiled the most interesting and useful information won the first part. The team that created the best "kill our business" plan won the second part. We tried to make the competition as much fun as possible, because annual planning is a particularly arduous part of the packaged goods calendar.

The results were amazing—to the point where I started to become concerned about legal liability. I was stunned to see how much we could learn about our competitors and their planning. In one case, a competitor was only too happy to lay out his plans in a "job interview" with a woman from our advertising agency. In another, a young R&D manager tromped around a competitor's construction site gathering some real gems from the workers.

The second phase was even more interesting. There's a huge difference between writing a page on a competitor and actually becoming that competitor and competing in a no-holds-barred way. The ten-point plans were creative and smart, and highlighted some key weaknesses on the home front. They were also very instructive in terms of the steps we needed to take—immediately—to ensure that they weren't put into place by our competitors.

Based on what we realized a smart, creative and active competitor might do against us, we set about the task of writing our own plans. As the year progressed, one of those competitors rolled out one tactic after another that we had predicted and planned for months earlier—to the point where I became convinced that someone on that team had actually leaked our plan to them. (Probably not but I never asked.) This was a competitor we felt was on its last legs anyway, and it exited the market before the end of the year. I like to think they gave up after they concluded we had a sixth sense that allowed us to anticipate their every move.

I *love* smart, ultra-competitive tactics. Another competitor, launching what we thought was a great new brand that could really hurt us, placed a lot of money behind a "trial marketing" program—i.e., giving away individual trial sizes to retailers and asking them to display the little boxes at 25 cents each (cheap for the consumer and pure profit for the retailer). We quickly ran a cost/benefit analysis and then asked all our able-bodied employees and their family members to go out and buy as many of those trial sizes as possible. Our competitor no doubt loved how quickly the trial sizes flew off the displays, but must have been quite puzzled by the dearth of repeat purchases. The brand didn't last the year.

Here's an interactive media question that was posed to me in the early days of Internet advertising: If a competitor is running an ad and paying every time someone clicks on that ad, should you have all of your employees, friends and relatives clicking like crazy on that ad to both drive your competitor's costs up and drive their conversion rate down? I can't believe that this was actually posed to me as a question! That said, don't bother. I don't think you can get away with this anymore; algorithms have caught up with those out to game the system.

Remember the Pepsi taste tests? Pepsi's marketers had limited success with cultured and creative campaigns, so they rolled up their sleeves and took out the brass knuckles. They ran a campaign that showed Pepsi beating Coke in blind taste tests—a truth that stemmed mostly from the fact that Pepsi was a bit sweeter and thus had a better "first sip" response. The campaign was successful for two reasons. First, it was ultra-competitive, harsh and attention-getting. It was Reality TV long before the term was even coined—low production values and everyday folks amidst a sea of expensively produced ads and professional actors.

Second, and perhaps more important, it made the other guy blink (the apt title of a subsequent book by Roger Enrico of Pepsi). Coke made the tragically misguided mistake of responding, first in advertising, then by launching "New Coke." All that managed to do was add fuel to a fire carefully selected and started by Pepsi. New Coke may have been a remarkably naïve move in its own right, but the seeds were sown by Pepsi and its taste test.

I love what Budweiser advertising did a few years ago. Miller had introduced an ad campaign featuring football refs taking Bud away from people and replacing it with Miller. Bud promptly countered with advertising showing police catching the refs running away with the stolen Bud, revealing that they planned to drink it themselves. Funny advertising, but it became hard to keep track of who was doing what to whom—an outcome I think Bud found more than acceptable. The Miller campaign then retreated to a less competitive (and seemingly less intrusive) plot. A trivial example, perhaps, but it shows how a dominant brand can make creative use of its power to remind the competition just who is in charge of the game.

Be competitive. Be very competitive. Be like Phil Knight of Nike. Assume there are only winners and losers, nothing in between. Or, to quote Yoda, one of my favorite philosophers: "Do or Do Not. There is no Try."

Be the competition—don't just talk about them. Don't like them, but do respect them. They're not statistics; they're a group of smart, creative people who want to eat your lunch. Eat theirs first.

54

Sir Isaac's First Law

Newton's Laws of Motion not only changed our view of the universe, they also make for very interesting reading for marketers.

His first law, governing inertia, tells us that if an object is in a certain state, it's very hard to change that state. Things tend to keep on doing what they've been doing. Marketers constantly underestimate Sir Isaac's first law—they underestimate the sheer power of inertia.

In order to move the marketplace you need to reach critical marketing mass. Do not underestimate what it takes to create change with a basically uninterested audience. Indeed, sometimes it seems impossible. As someone once said: "The only person who likes change is a wet baby." It's basic human nature; we feel comfortable with habit and we don't like to change our minds or our behaviors. On top of that, we're just not paying attention—especially not to opinions that contradict our own.

How's this for a stunning tribute to our unwillingness to change? Dr. Edward Miller, dean of medicine and CEO of the Johns Hopkins University hospital, followed the long-term progress of patients who had undergone heart surgery. Who could possibly have greater motivation to change lifestyle behavior than someone who has undergone heart surgery? But as Dr. Miller reported, "If you look at people after coronary-artery bypass grafting two years later, 90 percent of them have not changed their lifestyle." He goes on to say that "they know they should change their lifestyle [but] for whatever reason, they can't." At Northwestern Hospital, in fact, only 20 percent of heart surgery patients take a free rehabilitation program.

If a doctor can't motivate change after a life-threatening event, how easy can it be for a brand builder to change a customer's buying patterns through a marketing event?

Many marketers are completely unrealistic about what it takes to grab the attention of the marketplace and to create attitudinal or behavioral change. Real people have lives; they just don't care about a product or service the way a marketer (who is paid to care) does. Successful marketers learn to "de-focus"—i.e., pull back from what they're doing and what they know in order to make a realistic assessment of their chance of breaking marketplace inertia among people who aren't paying attention and have no real reason to change. Without this ability to de-focus, you run the risk of confusing a media plan, laid out on a piece of paper in isolation, and its implementation in real life, amidst a cluttered and competitive marketplace.

On the other hand, when change *naturally* occurs in the marketplace, it's an opportunity to break the inertia, and you have a chance to work that change to your advantage.

The mother of all inertia disruptions has been the growth of the Internet. And, while there have been thousands of flameouts, many very successful businesses have exploited this massive change to the status quo—think Google, Amazon, Expedia and eBay.

Similarly, Toyota saw a diminishing oil supply and higher fuel prices as an opportunity for its hybrid technology to break the inertia of the internal combustion engine.

Whole Foods has exploited our desire for something more natural, and brands such as Las Vegas and the cruise ship lines have exploited our post-9/11 preference for safe adventure.

We're also in the middle of a digital entertainment revolution, and the brand taking fullest advantage of the inertia break is, of course, Apple.

Windows of opportunity don't open all that often, so if you find one, for God's sake jump through it right *now*. Err on the side of too much force, because real opportunities don't come along that often and your brand has a unique chance to forever work from a significantly higher base just because you entered the market at the right time. There is nothing more disappointing than knowing a window was open but that you jumped too timidly or too late—and thus came up short.

Did Volkswagen spend too much launching the new Beetle when we all kind of knew it was coming? Would the Mini Cooper have been big even without that its great launch campaign? Did you finally get sick of seeing those great-looking Samsung print ads designed to make you reassess the Samsung brand as a design leader? Surely Apple didn't need to advertise the iPhone?

Better too much than too little, particularly when your entire future will be run from the level to which this program or campaign takes you.

Fortune absolutely favors the brave. History rarely provides a footnote for the timid.

55

Sir Isaac's
Second Law

Let's look at Sir Isaac Newton's law of motion:

"For every action there is an equal and opposite reaction."

Marketers love to look at trends. They love to listen to trend experts (who drive me crazy, seeming to define trends as "observations that don't demand action"). But what marketers don't do well is deal with actual real-world trends.

It is basic business theory that you need to ride marketplace momentum like a wave. So it goes without saying that finding and riding a trend can be great for business. But the fact that it is obvious also means that everyone is trying to do it—which rarely makes it a differentiating strategy. In other words, riding the wave of a hot trend is almost always a good thing . . . but may not always be the best thing.

Frankly, when it comes to trends, the creative side of my brain is much more intrigued by the "equal and opposite reaction" part of Sir Isaac's law. By that, I mean *for every trend, there will emerge one or more countertrends.*

For example, if the trend is everyone eating low-fat/low-cal, ride it if you can get on the leading edge—but know that everyone and their dog will be trying to ride it with you. So also look out for an opposite reaction: the "fatburger" (witness the success of Hardee's Monster Thickburger), the "triple-cheese pizza" and "super-rich ice cream." Yes, light beer seems more on-trend, but full-flavor, high-alcohol craft beers are doing very well, thank you.

Contrary to the physics of Sir Isaac's law, when it comes to business, the opposite reaction probably won't be equal; in fact, it'll likely result in something smaller. But there will be far fewer marketers trying to master it. If everyone's competing to have the lowest prices, go high end. If it's all about luxury, go Spartan. If everyone is building gas-guzzling SUV's, build a hybrid. Once everyone is building and buying hybrids, build a gas-guzzling monster truck. If everyone is pushing digital communication, push intimate handcrafted communication using high quality, sensuous paper and pens.

Look at it in terms of the "blue ocean, red ocean" construct: If you're not on that wave early, you're probably going to find yourself in a red ocean pretty quickly. Instead, look for the blue water. It may not qualify as an ocean, but sometimes high-margin smaller bodies of water are the places to be—and some even lead you to blue oceans that others don't see.

You can also stretch Sir Isaac's law into communications. It seems that almost every category tends to develop a verbal and visual language that permeates most of its marketing. Maybe it's because people are conservative and more comfortable doing what others do. Maybe it's because they're all looking at the same research, or because a strong leader takes one approach and others follow. But whatever the reason, at any point you can create a wall of category advertising and see how there's a certain sameness to the work. A language convention of some kind seems to be in play. Looks like a trend to me—so break it.

Make Sir Isaac proud.

56

Stop Fixing Things

If it works, push it. Push it hard.

This is a very simple, and therefore short, piece of advice. Too much management time is devoted to fixing things that are not going well. That's because no one likes to fail. If things are broken, our natural inclination is to fix them. To be clear, this is not an inherently bad thing—but it does have an opportunity cost.

Time spent improving or fixing things means less time devoted to taking complete and ruthless advantage of things that *are* going well. Ask yourself: What is working best? What are our real strengths? Where are we executing flawlessly? The natural tendency then is leave well enough alone. (If it ain't broke . . .)

But consider doing just the opposite. Look for ways to take even greater advantage of your strengths—and then drive that advantage home.

Sure, if something critical is broken, you've got to fix it. And if something less critical can be fixed easily, go right ahead. But sometimes things don't work because they're *not supposed* to work. Because they can't work. Because, no matter how well you do something, someone else can do it better.

They say that doing the same thing over and over and expecting a different result is a form of madness. In business, the more likely scenario is "I know it didn't work last year, but we'll execute it much better this year." If it didn't work before, don't try to fix it or make it better. Dump it and move on.

Stop what you're doing for a few minutes and consider your successes. Things work because they are the right things to do. Because they are supposed to work. So ask yourself a simple question: Can I make more of this?

True success just doesn't come along every day. When it does, squeeze every last drop out of it.

57

The Brand Hijack

Sometimes it's best to relax and enjoy the ride.

A t times the relationship between marketing (stimulus) and audience (response) is completely non-linear and seemingly random. Sometimes the audience decides for itself. When that happens, the product or service is "hijacked." (See Alex Wipperfurth's book, *Brand Hijack,* for deep and interesting thinking on this subject.)

Originally designed as a heavy-duty shoe and boot for the English "copper" (the British slang term for police officer), Doc Martens were hijacked by skinheads and turned into a symbol of rebellion against the establishment. When the Timberland and Cadillac Escalade brands were similarly hijacked by hip-hop, both companies were quick to realize and capitalize on their good fortune.

And how about the Portland bike messenger community hijacking Pabst Blue Ribbon? This case is interesting because the brand was hijacked due to the fact that it was cheap and because it had been abandoned by the mainstream. But failing to the point where you become an anti-mainstream icon is not exactly a recommended strategy. What do you do if you're the brand manager? You've been painted into a corner. That corner can widen, sure, but as soon as it gets to a certain size, it will disappear. As soon as PBR looks like it's on the cusp of becoming a "success," its community will walk away from it.

This is a reminder that getting hijacked isn't always a pleasant event. In the UK, Burberry was hijacked by a customer segment known—and not with affection—as the "chav" crowd. This decidedly downscale audience hurt the more upscale position of the Burberry brand; not surprisingly, Aristos quickly lost interest in a product showcased by an unconscious girl lying in the street and photographed in a newspaper tabloid. Closer to home for me, and while I wasn't looking, my beloved Jaguar XK8, which I think of as the sexy, sleek, modern equivalent of the classic E-type, was hijacked by a lot of folks who are . . .well . . . *old*.

What about when you do everything right but are still adopted by the "wrong" audience? Here are a couple of examples of exemplary product development and targeting work that nonetheless resulted in a completely unanticipated customer group.

The Honda Element offers a case study of how to build, from the ground up, a product around customer needs, in this case those of a college guy. The design team went on campuses, to the beach, to the hills—wherever college-age guys were living their active lives. They then built the Element in a minimalist fashion—like an automotive version of the Swiss Army Knife—taking into consideration every possible use a young adult male might have for it. They also did a perfectly good job of introducing the vehicle; it seemed obvious who was being targeted.

Surprise! The average age of the Element buyer? Forty-two.

Another great job in terms of brand development was LUNA, an energy bar specifically designed for active women. Well thought out, well packaged, well named and well marketed—all very clearly for women. Yet at one point, men actually accounted for more than 50 percent of purchases.

Both Element and LUNA were in some ways victims of their own success, and I'm a good example of what happened in both cases. Let's just say I'm considerably older than a college student and I'm not a woman. Yet I have been consistently tempted to buy an Element as a third vehicle—because we have a dog, because I bike every chance I get and because I find "low maintenance" to be a highly appealing proposition. I also regularly buy LUNA bars. I'm not sure how I got started, but perhaps it was as simple as liking the look, then liking the taste. (I'd like to think that it's because I'm in touch with my feminine side, but there are a lot of things that I'd like to think about myself . . . and most just aren't true.)

At the end of the day, the product itself is always king. You can position it, you can strategize it and you can market it, but if the product has no utility for me I'm not buying it. If the product has high utility for me, even if you try to disguise it or tell me it's for someone else, I'll find it and buy it anyway.

It's a pretty rare event, but if find yourself being hijacked and it's working for you, take a deep breath. Try to relax, because the hijacking may prove to be nothing more than random behavior and might not last. You need to find out what's really going on—but as a silent observer, not an active participant. If you get involved too early or too actively, you'll probably screw it up, no matter how deft you may be. Just keep an open mind and a sense of humor.

In *Brand Hijack*, Wipperfurth uses Mattel's management of its Barbie brand as a case study of what not to do. The Barbie community apparently loves to customize its dolls. But Mattel was so conservative and so stringent in its interpretation of appropriate "Barbie behavior" that the company sued, cajoled and otherwise alienated some of its most passionate brand advocates for behavior that it felt violated Mattel's "ownership" of this brand icon.

Compare the Mattel approach to Nike's. On March 30, 2005, the *New York Times Magazine* ran an article about entrepreneurs such as Mark Ong (a.k.a. "Sabotage") and an L.A. artist who prefers the moniker "Methamphibian." These guys were leading sneaker "customizers,"—meaning they used Nike shoes as canvases for their artwork. Nike could have become upset about this, as its designers spent a lot of time and money perfecting the Air Force 1s that these guys were messing with and selling for up to $900 a pair. But Nike "got it" in a way that Mattel never could, and left the artists alone (Nike wouldn't even comment for the *New York Times* story). The company also stayed out of the way of "Niketalk.com," a site created and managed by a group of sneaker fanatics.

Again, when your brand is hijacked and it's working against you, take a deep breath and relax. It may be your last chance to do so for a while. Do something about the hijacking if you can, but you'll have to be remarkably deft and it may be best to simply wait it out—and then pick up the pieces as fast as you can. As with so much of what I talk about, the real trick is to be so in tune with your marketplace and your customer that you see these "negative hijacks" coming and can act decisively before they gain any real momentum.

By and large, hijacking strikes are a random and therefore unpredictable act. It can be good for you or it can be bad for you, but most of its impact is largely beyond your control (though a lot marketers are called geniuses for what was, in fact, a good hijacking). Can you plan to be hijacked? I suppose it's possible, but I wouldn't spend a lot of time trying to figure out how. The act of hijacking and the act of planning don't really belong in the same universe. Stay in your own dimension.

58

Be Careful with the Brand Keys

A lot of knowledge can be a dangerous thing.

Retailers have become some of the best brand builders on the planet, a fact that may not bode well for their suppliers. The speed of the retail pulse and the hands-on relationship between retailer and customer make a great breeding ground for strong brands. As a result, retailers around the world have taken brand building to a whole new level over the past several years.

The retailer is closer to and generally knows the customer better than the manufacturer does. Clearly, this can work against the best interests of the manufacturer. Relationships are built on knowledge. If the retailer has the knowledge, and thus the relationship, he can guide brand choice within the store.

In one way, brands are good for retailers. They can command price (and margin) premiums and they can drive customers to the shelf. But in another way, strong manufacturer brands are against the best business interests of the retailer. Strong manufacturer brands rob the retailer of "degrees of freedom." Because they become brands that the retailer must have and can't switch out, they give the manufacturer leverage, and a supplier with leverage has never been a good idea from the retailer perspective.

If the retailer has the stronger customer relationship, it can vouch for brands and products in the store. "These jeans are just as good as Levi's but cheaper." "These corn flakes are just as good as Kellogg's but cheaper." Even worse: "These cookies are better, richer and have more chocolate chips than the leading brand." Strong U.S. retail brands such as Costco, Target and Wal-Mart, as well as Canada's Loblaws and Britain's Tesco and Sainsbury have raised this to an art form. And as shoppers, we love them for it.

From a manufacturing perspective, there is an increasing likelihood that you'll be dealing with retailers who have built stronger brands and stronger customer relationships than you have. And on top of this they still own the selling experience.

This point is more an observation than a piece of useful advice, but it does highlight the ongoing need for the manufacturer to build direct relationships with their customers (again, *not* consumers), particularly those they value most. The retailer may end up driving the car anyway, but be careful that you don't too easily hand over the keys. At the very least, make sure that you're in the passenger seat.

59

The New ROI—
Return on Imagination

Innovation creates a different form of ROI—a Return on Imagination.

Experience suggests to me that at any given point or moment, there are several big ideas residing within every organization that, if uncovered, would lead to significant top- and bottom-line growth.

These big ideas exist in minds that may not realize they're there, aren't aware of their potential or don't think they can win support. They exist in brands that have untapped equity and customer permission, as well as in products that can be improved and give birth to other products. Many of these innovations require little or no capital outlay; they are simple extensions of products, services and core skills that already reside within the organization. Clearly, there is no more profitable activity than the creation of revenue from assets that already exist.

We recently did an innovation project for a client who hadn't done any internal innovation for over a decade. We went into the project assuming that, after so many years, the employees would have plenty of pet ideas and frustrated projects. Looking for inspiration, our team interviewed numerous consumers and experts. We also put a lot of thought into the exercises we would use to structure a two-day offsite meeting with the client team, which was designed to turn insight into product ideas. To start everyone off, we set the participants up with virtual VC stake money, asking them what they would invest in if it were up to them.

The first hour of that offsite meeting resulted in an uninterrupted flow of great ideas. Our cup ran over, so much so that our team could barely keep up. In fact, so great was the quantity and quality of innovative ideas that we could have easily ended the two-day session right then and there.

Lesson learned. Make innovation an ongoing part of the company culture. Don't wait a decade. Hell, don't wait more than a year. Find ways to make small amounts of seed money available to "intrapreneurs" (regardless of department) to fund the exploration of worthwhile ideas. Let those with a passion for an idea keep ownership of it, at least in the early stages. And if it's a good idea, if it looks worthwhile, why not anoint the owner as "founder and CEO" of the project?

It is always important to remember that innovation is a creative act and to approach it accordingly. To quote Gary Hamel: "When it comes to innovation, the key point is [that] people get the courage to try new things not because they are convinced to do so by a wealth of analytical evidence but because they feel something *viscerally*. It's not that the analytics aren't important. It's just that until you feel something in your gut…you simply won't have the courage to act."

So feed the innovation engine. Have an ongoing conversation with consumers. Let them tell you what they think you should do. Such input seldom leads directly to a new product or service (consumers just aren't wired for innovation), but filtered through your experience and creativity, every now and then it might just lead to one of those Eureka! moments.

Again, as stated earlier, use all the analytical skills at your disposal. But at the end of the day, be ready to do something because it *feels* like you must. Invest in your employees' imaginations and you just might enjoy an unexpectedly large return.

60

Scenario-Based Planning—An Idiot's Guide

Forecasting the future is like driving a car blindfolded while following directions given by someone looking out the back window.

I love the concept of *scenario-based planning*. But most of us aren't ready to take the time or to spend the money required to do real scenario-based planning. Still, I think it's a great intellectual construct to borrow from.

Here's the idea. First, based on a ton of very sophisticated analytical work, create several future scenarios and describe how they relate to your endeavor. Assign to each of these possible futures an estimate of the probability of it representing the "real" future. Then describe everything you would do to take full advantage of (and mitigate against the issues created by) each of these specified futures.

Look at the indicated actions that you've created across all probable futures. What actions are called for under any and all of these futures? What actions are called for by all futures except the least probable? And so on, repeating this iterative process until you're left with only those actions called for by the least probable future.

Next, take all the actions called for across all futures and initiate them. A bit more judgment is required, but you also put into play most of the actions suggested by the majority of the high probability futures. Keep working down the list to determine which actions to take and which to place on hold pending specific milestones that might signal that the corresponding scenario could be in play.

While I love the concept and think everyone should at least go through a limited form of scenario-based planning as a conceptual framework, here's the rub: It is highly likely that the majority of your resulting "must do" list, while an essential foundation for growth, will not be differentiating in any way. And even if your strongest competitors don't go through the entire scenario-based planning process themselves, they are nonetheless likely to arrive at a similar set of conclusions.

What that means is that some competitive advantage may well be created, but only against the weak and dumb competitors, not against the smart and dangerous ones. Meanwhile, on the other end of the spectrum, you will have identified some highly explosive and differentiating actions that naturally tend to correspond to low probability futures. However, if you get even close to one of these future scenarios and have the action in place before it arrives, there is huge competitive advantage to be gained.

Let me admit that I know just enough on this subject to be dangerous. I'm an amateur scenario-based planner who happens to love the approach but lacks the attention span and analytical skills necessary to do it properly. But if you're like me, you might just want to pull together a smart, creative team and take the technique out for a test spin. If you find yourself even more intrigued after that test spin, find an expert and look into it further. I can't imagine a more decisive competitive advantage than to have your market make an unexpected turn that leaves all of your competitors flatfooted . . .while you have in your back pocket the perfect response.

61

Simplicity— The Ultimate Sophistication

I think it was Einstein who wanted everything to be made "as simple as possible, but not any simpler." Leonardo da Vinci saw simplicity as "the ultimate sophistication."

Think of a chart with two axes. The horizontal axis is time and the vertical is sweat. At the bottom left, where the two axes intersect at the (0,0) origin, is what I call *dumb simplicity*. We're all guilty of dumb simplicity. It's the immediate solution to a problem, without having really thought that problem through. If it's a small decision and you're experienced and actually good at what you do—then by all means go with dumb simplicity. For you, it's not so dumb, and since there are hundreds of these decisions lining up, just make one and move on.

Halfway out on both axes is *complexity*. After a bit of time and sweat, you've got a lot of information on your plate, and you're essentially "lost" in the input. Any important decision requires organizing input, building a framework and proposing hypotheses. But in the face of so much information, many (if not most) of us become stuck, lost in the complexity of data and details. We've developed structures to guide us, from the simplest SWOT analysis to complex scenario-based planning, but we get lost nonetheless. So here's what you need to remember: Decisions cannot be made at this stage. Decisions that are made at this stage are generally scary in nature and tragic in outcome.

Here's the other thing to remember: Keep looking. There, at the farthest reach of the two axes, where even more time and sweat have been expended, lies the genius of *true simplicity*. After working the input and fighting through the complexity, an elegantly simple solution is created. Simple in a telegraphic, focused and compelling way. Elegant in accounting for the most important information in a competitively advantageous and differentiated way.

True simplicity appears in almost every art and profession. In this case, I'm writing primarily with strategy in mind—the elegant simplicity of an intellectual solution to a marketing problem.

Increasingly, simple must be more than skin deep. Ideas, services and products that paint simplicity and elegance over a complex user experience may still create a competitive advantage, but any advantage will be short-lived. The iPhone, for example, is simple genius, whereas the Razr (sadly, for those of us who bought it) was merely elegantly designed. Underneath the sleek exterior of the iPod is an even more sleek operation and service. Underneath the sleek exterior of the Razr phone was just another complicated and non-intuitive user interface. Similarly, you may not love the look of the Prius, but there's no question that its design is elegantly simple, and that its simplicity is built-in from the ground up.

Simple can be dumb. Simple can be genius. Complex is just complex.

62

Our Infatuation
with Cool

Either you're cool
or you aren't.

A client asked me to pull together a presentation for its marketing team that would show them "how to be cool." This was funny on two fronts. The first laugh is that anyone would ask me to talk about being cool. The second is based on the fact that (as I told them) if you need to ask how to be cool, by definition you cannot be cool.

Cool is one of those overused marketing terms. Yet being cool seems to be viewed as an end unto itself by many marketers, rather than as just one possible means to an end.

When I worked at Ogilvy & Mather in Chicago, I had the pleasure of working with a guy named Ray Lyle, who headed up production at the agency. Ray was, and I'm sure still is, cool. He once said something at a meeting that struck me; I don't remember what it was, and it actually doesn't matter. I did a double take and asked him how the hell he had become so cool. Ray didn't even blink. He just sat back in his chair and said, in his oh-so-cool baritone: "I don't know, Austin. I guess I've just always been this way." It wasn't a boast, it wasn't a joke—it was a simple statement of fact.

As a brand, Ray Lyle is cool. As a brand, Austin McGhie is not cool. In general, brands are cool because they are. Because of who or what they are. Cool is a natural state, not one that can be manufactured. In fact, the very act of trying to be cool automatically defines you as not cool. Cool is a response from your audience, not a stimulus from you. Brands that we like to think of as cool are brands that are singular, that dare to be different, and that aren't afraid of polarizing their audiences. Cool brands, like people, are totally and obviously comfortable in their own skin.

I once had an interesting chat with the folks who run Red Bull in the U.S. There was a rumor going around that one of the active ingredients in Red Bull comes from bulls' testicles—a characteristic that some might find a bit off-putting. I asked the Red Bull people whether this was true. (It isn't.) I then asked if they were doing anything to counter the misunderstanding. The Red Bull brain trust just smiled one of those "he doesn't get it yet" smiles and shook their heads. Their brand isn't a model citizen, but it's one with real personality, one that comes with a bit of a dark side. And these people are clearly comfortable in their brand's skin.

In the mid 1990s, two new small cars vied for the attention of American youth. One—I can't remember the brand name—spent a lot of time trying to create an empathetic relationship with teens, using just about every piece of just slightly out-of-date jargon the ad agency could muster. The hero in the spot was painfully hip. The other brand, the Geo, simply told the audience, straight out, why they should buy it and how much it cost, all within a minimalist approach that focused totally on the car. Who won? Well, there's a reason I can't remember the other brand.

So don't chase cool; it will either come to you or it will not. Be yourself, dare to be different and have the courage of your convictions, and the odds are good that cool may just show up on your doorstep. But don't pursue it. And remember that lots of things are cool to a fully informed customer. Superior performance and utility, for example, can be very cool indeed. As I said, kids today will tell you that Microsoft is pretty cool. Why? Because it offers them high utility. Microsoft works for them.

Cool is also not an inherently desirable characteristic. Remember that so-called cool brands, while fun to talk and write about, tend to be on the smaller end of the business scale. It's tough to be big and stay cool. There are exceptions, of course. Apple and Nike have certainly managed it, Starbucks still does pretty well for such a well-distributed brand, and Twitter and Google are still going strong. But no one ever mentions MySpace these days, and Facebook, while still increasing its audience, is losing its edge. At the end of the day, big does not coexist comfortably with cool, so the list really isn't that long. Cool ubiquitous brands are rare.

So don't try to fake it, particularly if your audience is young. They'll sniff you out in a heartbeat. Teenagers are the smartest customers, and they have a very finely tuned bullshit meter. A "not cool" from them can be the kiss of death.

63

Technology Marketing—It's Different Out There

I t's time to debug this brand strategy stuff so that a technology marketer can use it.

I admit to a particular fascination with the marketing of technology. It may be the sense of possibility, or it may be the sense of invention. It may simply be that this industry seems to be filled with smart, intense people who generally don't spend a lot of time thinking about marketing and brands.

The art and science of positioning applies regardless of category, but the marketing of technology is undeniably different. Here are a few of the more significant differences to ponder.

First, you have an entire *customer ecosystem* to manage. Unlike the much simpler product/consumer relationship found in the packaged goods world, you've got to market to and manage an interactive ecosystem of customers, employees, channel partners, competition, analysts and the press. It's like a cocktail party; while having a conversation with just one audience, you need to stay alert to the fact that the others are probably listening over your shoulder. Each conversation is unique, but there must also be a central theme. And positioning your technology brand or business isn't optional, If you don't position yourself firmly within this ecosystem, other "partygoers" will be more than happy to do it for you.

Second, the notion of momentum or "riding the wave" is particularly important to the technology marketer. It's simple enough in theory but complicated in practice. Pick the wrong wave and you'll waste a lot of energy and—more important in this fast-moving world—time. Pick the right wave but fail to grab clear ownership of a piece of it and you'll have to give way to another "surfer." Get too far forward on the wave (especially in this economy) and you can outrun the underlying technology. Get too far back and you'll be left behind. And through all of this the wave moves on, constantly changing speed and shape.

Brand momentum was defined earlier in this book as marketplace perception that is moving toward you, rather than away from you. Momentum marketing is also likened to the running of a political campaign, or hand-to-hand combat. In technology marketing we can learn a lot from the political campaigners, particularly in terms of the "war-room" mentality. In the business-to-business marketing model, the service that sits behind the product can be more critical to the "sell" than the product itself. Industry standards may also be involved. Meanwhile, the risk inherent in a bad purchase decision can be extremely high, so the purchaser tends toward the safe bet—the momentum bet.

Third on our list is the importance of *timing*. Timing is always important to the marketer, but can and will make or break the technology marketer. Most smart technology marketers can paint a picture of the future that is pretty accurate. Most can get you to nod your head and say, "Yes, I can see how that will happen." The better ones also do a good job of placing their product or service into an enabling or fairly central role in that future. All of this is important, all great stuff—but it's the ones who both see the future and get the schedule right that make the big money. Most of us get the idea that one day we'll be enjoying video and audio entertainment from a mobile computer/television entertainment center, using the Internet as the transmission medium to access limitless content from around the world. Most of us get the idea that our cell phones will be used to access a world of entertainment options and location-based services. There is no news in any of this.

The trick is "owning" a piece of these shifts, however small that piece may be. The next trick is in getting the schedule right. Timing really can be everything.

Fourth, you've got to seriously consider the notion that great brands are built from the inside out. Go to school on brands like Apple, Amazon and Google. But also look at some of the non-technology brands mentioned elsewhere. Technology companies simply haven't been the best breeding ground for strong and differentiated brand cultures—mainly because the marketing thing tends to be bolted on as an afterthought. Technology is full of incredibly bright people filled with energy and purpose, but is generally not driven by marketing. While it relies on a thorough analytical underpinning, the best marketing is still intuitive and creative in nature, which flies in the face of the intellectual rigor demanded in all other areas of the technology business. It follows, then, that marketing must somehow become a critical driver for the technology company rather than the afterthought it is today.

As you think this all through, here are some of the topics in this book that I think warrant special consideration by the technology marketer.

- Start with a differentiated business proposition
- Niche is not a four-letter word, especially in technology markets
- Be an owner, not a player

- Keep it real
- Think: inertia, critical marketing mass and the importance of change
- Short cycle times require adaptive strategies
- Think: Customer Relationship Management (CRM)

All of which brings me to one last thought (or personal peeve, depending how you look at it) for the business-to-business technology marketer:

Years ago I was asked to help a major technology player with its marketing strategy. This company was spending well north of $100 million to advertise its brand, primarily on television. I asked a fairly innocuous question: How many people in the world actually buy or influence the purchase of the technology you sell? Given the high dollar value of the company's products and services, the answer was "a thousand or so."

Let's think about this. You are selling to a group that numbers a thousand or so. You have their names and addresses. You know where they work. Why on earth aren't you spending your advertising budget to directly intercept them as they go about their daily lives? Yes, you're building a brand, and it's great that you can reach millions of people who might, someday, somehow, be involved in some way with your product or service. But touching millions doesn't remotely have as much value as actually catching the attention of thousands of decision makers.

You're trying to build a business, and brand building is simply one of the available tools. Building that brand with people who will never buy your product has some utility (the cocktail party), but it's a luxury most of us cannot afford.

Here's an example of an alternative approach. Talk to a major media player, say Time Warner. Have the sales department give you the names and occupations of the few thousand people who might actually help you build your business. Ask Time Warner to isolate these people on their subscription lists, adding publications where necessary (offered free to the target audience). Then, instead of single-page ads to millions, you're in the position to place cover wraps and six-page spreads to thousands. Everyone wins. The audience (the *real* audience) gets a bunch of free magazines with content they're interested in, and you actually get noticed (in a big and consistent way and at a lower total cost). Add some targeted outdoor advertising that sits in a highly visible position on commutes to and from work, and away you go.

Finally, if you're reading this and you're a technology marketer, I'm willing to bet you are a smart and highly analytical problem solver. I'm also willing to bet that you've now dissected my book and have a long list of questions I'd have to struggle to answer. If so, I sincerely hope you'll accept the notion that marketing is art built atop science. It's analytical for sure, but if you want to win through marketing you'll also need to be inventive, intuitive and creative.

If you run a technology company, find room in that company for a real marketer.

64

Positioning You

gain, let's forget the B word for a minute. People are products, too, and need to be effectively positioned. As mentioned elsewhere, positioning happens—so if you don't position yourself, others are more than happy to do it for you. Just look at politics for the proof of this statement.

Here's an exercise that is mentioned elsewhere in this book but bears repeating. Take a ruthlessly honest look at yourself. Disassemble the elements that contribute to brand "you" and write out your constituent equities. Ask those who know you well to review and edit the list.

Now, break that list into three categories:

- Identifiers: what defines and differentiates you

- Contributors: what is integral to your brand but that isn't defining

- Passengers: what holds you back and restricts your potential

Build your position out of your identifiers. What is the one idea that you'd like to be known for?

Take a ruthless look at your passengers. They are, after all, holding you back. Does your position address them in a way that can reduce their "drag coefficient"? Can it? If not through promoting your position, can you simply minimize them through focused effort?

Remember Batman? His passengers included his age (perceived by kids as over forty—ancient!), his butler (even older) and his choice in real estate (a dark, spooky mansion). His key identifier was the fact that he, alone among his peer group, went out and built his powers. At the center of the positioning strategy was the defining phrase: *From purpose comes power.* Given that this initial work was already done, Warner Brothers has done a pretty great job of making him younger, showcasing how he got those powers and building the back-story in a way that kids today can relate to.

You can't be Batman, but you can be a super-hero, if only to your parents and dog.

Conclusion

*"Art is a passion pursued
with discipline and
science is a discipline
pursued with passion."*

—Arthur M. Sackler

I continue to be fascinated by this combination of art, science and commerce that we call marketing, and I hope that this fascination has resulted in a book you find useful.

A few final thoughts:

Be *analytical*—it's insane to make important decisions without looking at the situation from all sides. Know your subject matter and your customer's psyche better than anyone else.

Be *courageous*. Maybe you're not the next Steve Jobs, but try acting like it anyway. And if yours is organization that doesn't celebrate courage, find one that does.

Be *creative*. You can pretty much assume that everyone out there will connect the dots with straight lines. So go free form instead. Paint pictures that connect the dots. Move those damn dots around to better suit your purpose.

Be *passionate*. Most people work because they must but you're in a position to love what you do. If you don't love what you do, whatever "it" might be, you will never be really good at it.

It's called marketing, not risk management. Be a marketer. Get famous. Build a spectacularly successful business. Then be sure to attribute all of your success to this book.

Thanks in advance.

A User's Guide to the User's Guide

Sixty-plus chapters!

That's a lot of ideas spread out throughout a lot of sections. So, assuming you'll come back to this book one of these days to clarify a point you vaguely remember, here's a brief summary of the chapters. If you don't find what you're looking for here, you will at least know where to go to find the longer discussion.

A busy marketer who doesn't have time to read (or re-read) every single carefully written word can skim the next few pages and extract much of the wisdom I have to convey.

But if you are just thumbing through this section at the bookstore . . . at least buy the damn book!

1. Introduction
Why did he write this?

2. Brand (Double) Speak
A brief review of the often-nonsensical language of "branding."

3. What the Hell is a Brand Anyway?
Brand is one of the most abused words in the business lexicon. What does it really mean to today's marketer? More important, what does it really mean to today's consumer?

4. Great Brands Are Built from the Inside
Great positioning guides and inspires both those inside the company and the outside audience. But you've got to guide and inspire your organization before they in turn can guide and inspire your customers. Build the position into the culture and the culture into the position. Get the position out of the marketing department and infuse it throughout the company. Use it to direct behavior. Live the position— and only then introduce it to the rest of the world.

5. Want a Great Brand? Build a Great Product

You can only sell sizzle for so long. Sooner or later the customer has to sit down and eat. Marketing communications are critically important, but they are no substitute for a superior customer experience. This may seem a blinding glimpse of the obvious, but too many of us like to ignore its truth. Talk to the smartest consumer on the planet (any teenager will do) about a brand and he or she will tell you about product performance.

6. A Brand is a Response, Not a Stimulus

Many marketers talk about brands as if they can simply buy one. Unfortunately for them, brands are a marketplace response, not a marketer's stimulus. Smart marketers realize that their strategies and plans not only need to be coherent and consistent, but that this stimulus will travel through the medium of a consumer's head, bounce around in there with a lot of other stuff, then come back as a response. If that response is simple, clear and on strategy, you may just build yourself a brand.

7. Differentiation—Often Discussed, Seldom Achieved

It has been proven that strong businesses and brands are built through *differentiation*—a term that is simple in concept but incredibly difficult in practice. It takes real daring to be different. Perhaps that's why so many great brands were built by cranky entrepreneurs who were more than happy to ignore conventional wisdom.

8. Difference Must Be More Than Skin Deep

Contrary to standard practice, differentiation is not something that marketing can "bolt on" to a product or service. It has to be built in from the start—often as far back as in the design lab. You must start with a truly differentiated business proposition if you want to build a truly differentiated brand.

9. Eccentricity Rules

Perhaps differentiation is too mild a word for today's cluttered marketplace. Perhaps it's time to become more "eccentric"—more contrary and radical—in how we approach brand and business positioning.

10. Differentiated Advantage

Without a doubt, it all starts with difference—but there are many ways to be different. In fact, any idiot can be different. The trick is to be different in a way that is highly relevant to your audience. Different in a way that creates competitive advantage. Advantage that is, over time, as sustainable as possible. All of which is to say—it's not easy. Difference + Advantage = Differentiated Advantage.

11. The Importance of the Missionary Position

Some of our greatest brands are built around a sense of shared passion. This shouldn't be surprising: consumers and customers naturally want to feel a sense of shared mission about the brand; that we, too, have contributed to its success. And in a lonely world, we've never needed that sense of mission more than we do today. When we purchase a product or service, we aren't just buying it, we are buying *into* it—and we want that commitment reciprocated.

12. Don't Be a Prisoner

Defining the business you're in isn't as simple as it seems and it can have incredibly far-reaching implications. It's remarkably easy to become a prisoner of your own point of view, particularly if you've been successful. Regularly challenge your business definition by finding a few radical thinkers to force you out of your comfort zone. Challenge your business definition before others do.

13. Invent, Don't Construct.

If the key is differentiation, how do you get there? True difference is invented, not constructed. Yes, market information and customer analysis are important, but they're also business commodities. Sooner or later, you've got to make an intuitive leap if you really want to be different.

14. Love Me or Hate Me—Just Don't Like Me

Great brand positions polarize. Like great people, you either love or hate them, but you certainly can't ignore them. For businesses that are terrified to offend anyone, this is often a tough truth to swallow.

15. Position Narrow, Catch Wide

This is another form of separating stimulus from response. The tighter the position, the stronger the position. This may be counterintuitive to those who think you need a broad message to gain a broad audience, but people who think that way aren't actually marketers.

16. Own Something

In the world of marketing, it's not enough to be a player. You need to be an *owner*. It might be a market "space." It might be a compelling idea. It might be a position. But whatever you call it, you'd better own it. Be famous for something—or get used to the world of discount pricing.

17. Niche is Not a Four-Letter Word

A niche can be a highly profitable place from which to view the world. Several niches can add up to one very large and profitable business. In marketing, "broad" is much more a four-letter word than is "niche."

18. The Joys of Disruption

Markets can change direction. They can be re-invented. They can splinter. When these market discontinuities occur, new "owners" are born. See it coming and grab the opportunity. Better still, create a disruption of your own.

19. The Disposable Strategy

There is one characteristic of change that no one can deny: it *happens*. It might be planned. It might be completely unexpected. But change will happen. That means if we are going to escape strategically painting ourselves into a corner, we must build marketing strategies that are flexible enough to allow for change. So what's the "disposal cost" of your strategy?

20. Positioning Happens

Positioning is not an optional activity. If you don't actively and aggressively position your business, others will be more than happy to do it for you . . . and you won't like the result. As the saying goes, if you don't know where you're going, any road will take you there.

21. Find Your Difference

If you're buying into all of this differentiation stuff, here's a repeat of my warning that any idiot can be different. You need to find the things that make you both different and compelling to your audience, and to use what you find in ways that create advantage over your competition.

22. Brand Architecture—A Positioning Puzzle

Think of architecture as an organizational chart that represents one big positioning puzzle. Position each box on the chart so as to make its difference compared to the other boxes clear. Each box also has its own competitive set and your job is to figure out how to differentiate it in a way that creates clear advantage against those competitors. Then help your audience navigate that organizational chart as easily and intuitively as possible. Architecture can both attract and retain. It can also act to guide you as you build your portfolio.

23. The Non-Sense of Positioning

Great positions speak to the supporting organization. They direct behavior. But a lot of money changes hands in the name of "brand positioning," and a lot of that dough is wasted on frivolous poetry that has no real business value or inherent competitive advantage.

24. Build Critical Marketing Mass

The most common marketing mistake is to assume that the marketplace is paying attention. To believe that a message sent out is a message received. But ask yourself: how many of your emails each day do you actually open? It is incredibly (let me repeat: incredibly) hard to break through all the noise and clutter and be noticed, especially among strangers. Yet many marketers spread their money around in a way that actually ensures they will never be heard. You may need to be creative to get there, but if you can't generate critical marketing mass, you are wasting your money.

25. Stop Thinking Outside the Box

Any idiot can think outside the box. Just as even the most unimaginative manager can easily stay in the middle of the box—on strategy, yes, but uninspired and therefore unnoticed. Great marketers realize that their job is to punch the hell out of the edges of the box, because that's the only way to change the size of that box, to make the box bigger.

26. Change

Think of the marketplace as a downward-moving escalator. If you stand still, you're actually going down. So run, don't walk! Find the news. Talk to your customers. Stay ahead of the game. Change what you've been doing, but be careful; change is a two-edged sword.

27. Find the Flow

Momentum marketing is something that political campaigners have long understood better than we "sophisticated" brand builders. Put simply, you either ride real marketplace momentum or create some momentum of your
own—because you really can't fight momentum when it's
working against you. When it comes to momentum, commercial brand builders need to build a sustainable version
of the political "war-room" and "action-reaction" mentality
into our approach.

28. Think Before You Blink

If someone (an author, perhaps) tells you that marketing
needs to be more analytical, that someone has it half right.
If someone else (another author, perhaps) tells you that you
need to go with your gut, that person also has it half right.
Put those halves together and you have a whole marketing
philosophy (and just one book instead of two).

29. Build an Experience

A position is a de facto promise of a customer experience.
That becomes obvious when you are managing an immersive
or experiential service, but perhaps not so obvious if you're
marketing a box of corn flakes. When you treat your product
as an experience, it can enhance your position—and make
for happier customers.

30. Make Yourself Famous

Too many marketers are simply putting in time. Too many
marketers are hoping for the good result rather than going
all-out for the spectacular result. The problem with spectacular
success, however, is that it can only be gained at the risk of spectacular failure. Nonetheless, it's good to be ambitious. Go ahead
and get famous. Your business will thank you for it.

31. The Consumer is Dead

Splitting hairs? Perhaps, but the word "consumer" implies some form of shapeless purchasing mass rather than a unique, thinking and feeling "customer." It's time to start thinking about our sensate customers and leave mindless consumption behind.

32. Your Consumer is a Cynic

Blame it on the Internet. Blame it on the media or the school system. Blame it on Enron or Solyndra. Blame it on marketers who over-promise and under-deliver. You can even blame it on the government. Blame it on whomever and whatever you want, but all that really matters is that your consumer has become a professional cynic and you need to deal with that reality.

33. Saints and Sinners

Simply put, divide your audience into saints, sinners and undecideds. Your saints are going to buy you anyway; they need to be treated well and, if possible, turned into brand advocates. Your sinners aren't going to buy your product no matter what you do, so why waste money talking to them? Instead, spend a lot more time focusing on the undecideds. Get to know these fence sitters really well because the side of the fence they choose can make or break you.

34. Customers Not Marketing Advisors

There is a critical order to the marketing of things. First, figure out the position that will maximize the competitive opportunity. Then talk to your customers and get their "permission" to ask them what they need. Ultimately, it's your ability to bring your business needs and your customers' needs together that will determine your success. But always start with your business. You're in this to create competitive advantage, not simply to please your customers.

35. Are You Feeling It?

The best research almost always occurs in the real world. But marketers, who for the most part live in nice homes in a few big cities and hardly ever ride the bus, are rarely aware of how far removed they are from real customers. Fewer research dollars should go toward the generation of data and more toward immersing those marketers in the real world of the company's real audience.

36. Drowning in Information

We are drowning in information. In the Internet age we are all Ancient Mariners—all that water but nothing we can drink. The good news is that marketing isn't powered by information; it's powered by insight. Yes, information is an essential precursor to insight, but beware a tendency to get so busy analyzing information that you don't have time left over to formulate real insights.

37. The Importance of Why

You don't need a Ph.D. in psychology to know that people hold beliefs and engage in behaviors for reasons a lot deeper than "because I saw an ad." Get to know your audience outside of their engagement with your product or service. Understand their hopes, fears, ambitions, attitudes and points of view. Better yet, *talk* to them, on a regular basis, and stay away from all that marketing crap—it can come later.

38. I Like to Watch

One of the most enduring observations about human behavior is that *people don't always do what they say.* So try this: spend time on a regular basis watching real people approach, purchase and use your product as a part of their daily lives. Watch what they do with it—and only then ask them why.

39. Do You Know How High is Up?

We do lots of test marketing, but have you ever taken the time to create a vision of your "perfect market"? You owe it to your business to know how high is up—if for no other reason than to realize just how far you have to go (or, conversely, just how low that ceiling really is). Do whatever it takes to get all the variables right, even if on a very small front. Then calculate the upper limit of your business. It can be a real eye-opener.

40. Keep It Real

A product really is worth a thousand words. Too many marketing campaigns are purely conceptual in nature. They spend a lot of money just to sell us on an idea, when all we really want to know is why we should buy a product or service and get on with our lives.

41. What's Your Back-Story?

Think of your marketing communication effort as a frontstory. If possible (and it's often not) that front-story should be grounded in a clear, brand-based back-story. An active and compelling back-story serves as a continuing narrative, making the brand marketer's job that much easier. So think of your product as a character actor in need of a clear and compelling back-story. Who is this character? Where did he come from? What propels him?

42. Attention—The New Brand Currency

Consumer attention has become a scarce resource. Then why are so many of our methods and so much of our research still rooted in a time when attention was assumed and persuasion was the order of the day?

43. The Dollar Value of Creativity

Keep in mind that it's only great strategy if it makes for great tactics. Think of creativity as a strategic multiplier. Creative strategies are marketable ideas in their own right—provocative, intriguing and capable of gathering a lot more of that scarce marketplace attention than they otherwise might deserve. The same approach holds for tactics. Find and overpay truly creative people to translate that provocative strategy into clever, attention-getting communication.

44. A Nod to David Ogilvy

David Ogilvy took a lot of bashing thanks to a bunch of superficial and creatively precious types who took his insistence that advertising sells products as somehow "anti-creativity." David actually loved creativity—but prized only the more difficult, intelligent and effective kind. Strangely enough, be abhorred the stupid, oversimplified articulation of creativity. He stood for creativity that works. You should too.

45. Assume You'll Only Get One Shot

Far too many marketers spend money simply because it's in the budget. Because it's in the plan and it's time to spend it. And because they feel competitive pressure to be "out there." Well, *stop*. Don't spend a dime until you get it perfect. Push your partners to help you get it perfect. It's hard to do, but you've got to be willing to stop the train . . . even if the schedule says that it's time to leave the station.

46. Advertising—And the Need for Radical Re-engineering

The marketplace can be like a very fast jet: by the time you hear it, it's already passed you by. Similarly, the concept of the advertising agency "middleman" as a business model is increasingly out of step with the times. Having been slow to respond to massive sea changes taking place within their businesses, agencies must adopt the attitude of smart tech companies and (quickly) reinvent their business model.

47. Marketing in a World of Ubiquitous Information

In the past, we used brands as navigational devices. They helped us avoid the confusion of choice—a valuable service in a world where facts were hard to come by. Today, those same facts are ubiquitous, available anytime and anywhere at the touch of a keypad. In the face of this information revolution, the role of the brand must change.

48. It Takes a Village to Raise a Brand

Great brands are built as much (if not more) by their audiences as their purveyors. Find your village, learn its culture and embrace the village elders. Listen closely to the villagers and you will be repaid many times over.

49. The Truth Will Win Out—Sooner Not Later

The age of bamboozling customers is long gone. Modern audiences, armed with the Internet, can very easily match our arguments and products against reality. So, assume that the truth will win out—and make an honest assessment of where this fact of life will leave you and your business.

50. Catch a Virus

Word of mouth has always been the most effective way to build a business, and now it's a technique on steroids. Thanks to the Web, word-of-mouth marketing has been accelerated. Use that fact to your advantage. Build your marketing "virus," but build it carefully and build it around the truth. That takes patience, soft hands and a deft touch, but it'll be worth it in the end.

51. Market to the Brand Broadcaster

Each of us carries a "broadcast index," i.e., a measure of our propensity to actively broadcast our brand choices to those around us. In many business categories, finding the most influential broadcasters can produce great marketing efficiencies. The challenge is not just to find those broadcasters, but also to find a way to recruit them to your side.

52. Marketing is Judo, Not Karate

No one will ever get rich trying to change the mind of the marketplace. Think judo. Find out what your audience thinks and where the natural marketplace momentum lies. Then, figure out how to leverage it to your advantage. Go with the marketplace flow and bend it to your purpose—don't try to fight it. Instead, use its massive strength to your advantage.

53. If It's Not Important Enough to Win, You'll Lose

If you're not intensely competitive, you will never be much of a marketer. It's a dog-eat-dog world out there, and you want to be the one doing the dining. This is not a time for politics or niceties. Get out there and kick some ass.

54. Sir Isaac's First Law

Sir Isaac Newton's first law tells us that if an object is in a certain state, it's very hard to change that state. Enterprises (like people) tend to keep on doing what they've been doing. As marketers, we are paid to find ways to violate Sir Isaac's law, but we underestimate the strength of that law at our peril.

55. Sir Isaac's Second Law

Newton's second law states that "for every action there is an equal and opposite reaction." In marketing, this law can be creatively translated into a suggestion to look at the prevailing trend and then imagine what an exploitable countertrend might look like. With the marketplace, the opposite reaction usually results in a smaller payoff, but that payoff can also be more "ownable," as well as more profitable, for whoever captures it.

56. Stop Fixing Things

It's a human characteristic. If something isn't working the way we think it should, we want to fix it. In business, we generally face a range of actions, some of which are working, some of which are not. Consider showing the door to things that aren't working and focusing on things that are working. Make life binary. If it's broke, don't fix it—unless it's mission-critical that the problem be set right. If it's working, throw more weight behind it.

57. The Brand Hijack

Sometimes consumers just don't get the memo and a bunch of them decide to define and use your brand in a way that can damage it. Other times, the hijack is actually positive and works to your advantage, at least in the short-term. Hijacking is a relatively rare event, but you still have to guard against it—even as you are prepared to take advantage of it.

58. Be Careful with the Brand Keys

Retailers are becoming great marketers and brand builders, building trust among customers and establishing a much closer relationship than most manufacturers enjoy. That's good for them—but not necessarily for the manufacturers. Consider this: if your customer trusts the retailer more than you, what happens if that retailer endorses a product that is "just as good but cheaper" than yours?

59. The new ROI—Return on Imagination

At any given moment there are several big ideas hidden within any organization. They exist in minds that may not even realize they're there, aren't aware of their potential, or don't think they can win support. They exist in products with untapped customer equity and permission, and in products that can improve themselves or give birth to other products. There is no more profitable activity than the leveraging of assets that already exist. Do you have an established system to identify and nurture these hidden ideas?

60. Scenario-Based Planning—An Idiot's Guide

Someone once described forecasting as driving a car blindfolded while following directions given by someone looking out the back window. This section is a layman's guide to how to forecast the future and to use that forecast to your advantage.

61. Simplicity—The Ultimate Sophistication

Leonardo da Vinci saw simplicity as "the ultimate sophistication," but he neglected to warn us that simplicity has many forms. For marketers, simplicity exists on both sides of complexity. Don't settle for "dumb simplicity" and don't get stuck in complexity. Fight through that complexity to find a solution that represents elegant simplicity.

62. Our Infatuation with Cool

You are either cool or you are not, and it's not worth chasing something you can't ever catch. I know people who are cool and I know brands that are cool—and neither was the result of conscious effort. If you have to ask how to be cool, you never will be cool. And here's the good news: for the newest generation of consumers, a product is cool if it works really well. Elegant simplicity of look and operation is, by definition, cool. Give that age cohort a truly great product or service and they'll take it from there.

63. Technology Marketing—It's Different Out There

I guess you could make this argument for any number of categories, but technology is the one I'm most fascinated with. So here's a unique set of marketing considerations for a very unique and dynamic sector, one that's driven more by marketing than most people realize.

64. Positioning You

You can apply a lot of this thinking to your personal brand. A simple exercise allows you to apply the process of positioning to yourself with ruthless honesty. Conduct your own market research with the audience that matters most to you. Then disassemble and organize your "equities" so that you can both build your position and minimize anything that will slow the rapid ascent that will inevitably occur once you start putting the principles in the book into practice.

About the Author

Austin McGhie is the president of Sterling Brand's Strategy Group. Throughout his thirty-year career, he ran marketing departments, sales forces and advertising agencies before slowly coming to the realization that he was really only good at strategy. Austin fervently believes that there is no marketing problem or opportunity that can't be framed as a positioning exercise. Austin's team at Sterling Brands works with some of the top marketers in the world, including Disney, ESPN, Nike, Google, Visa, Expedia, Best Buy, Microsoft, Anheuser-Busch, Abbott and YouTube.

Austin thinks he is a brilliant marketing strategist. Those who work with him agree, though they tend to be somewhat dependent on him financially, so they may just be telling him what he wants to hear. Everyone who knows him—including all his clients—agrees that he thinks he's a brilliant strategist. When asked to comment for this book, Alpa Pandya, who heads up Sterling's strategy practice in New York, actually called him "the Michael Jordan of marketing strategy." One of his favorite clients, Sharon Otterman, chief marketing officer at MSNBC said, "He forces you to re-think things, refusing to play along and not hesitating to take a stand, even if it's counter to yours." If she'd had the time, she might have argued that this "stand" often actually made sense.

Austin travels too much, but when he's home he lives in Northern California's Marin County with his wife, two children and dog. Back in the day, he was "almost good enough" to play professional soccer. Having recently ridden his bike across the country, you can usually find him riding up the nearest hill.

Index

N

O

P

Q

R

T

U

V

How can you use this book?

MOTIVATE

EDUCATE

THANK

INSPIRE

PROMOTE

CONNECT

Why have a custom version of *Brand Is A Four Letter Word?*

- Build personal bonds with customers, prospects, employees, donors, and key constituencies
- Develop a long-lasting reminder of your event, milestone, or celebration
- Provide a keepsake that inspires change in behavior and change in lives
- Deliver the ultimate "thank you" gift that remains on coffee tables and bookshelves
- Generate the "wow" factor

Books are thoughtful gifts that provide a genuine sentiment that other promotional items cannot express. They promote employee discussions and interaction, reinforce an event's meaning or location, and they make a lasting impression. Use your book to say "Thank You" and show people that you care.

Brand is A Four Letter Word is available in bulk quantities and in customized versions at special discounts for corporate, institutional, and educational purposes. To learn more please contact our Special Sales team at:

1.866.775.1696 • sales@advantageww.com • www.AdvantageSpecialSales.com